PRINCIPLES OF SELF-MANAGEMENT

PRINCIPLES OF SELF-MANAGEMENT

The Key to Personal and Professional Success

John C. Marshall, PhD / Bob McHardy, CLU

Self Management Group / Toronto

Canadian Cataloguing in Publication Data

Marshall, John C., Ph.D
    The principles of self-management

ISBN 0-9682287-2-0

1. Self-management (Psychology).
2. Self-actualization (Psychology). 3. Success.
I. McHardy, Bob. II. Title.

BF637.S4M368 1999   158.1   C99-930423-2

PREFACE

About the Authors

John C. Marshall, the president of Self Management Resources Corporation and a principal of the P.L.U.S. Corporation, has a PhD in psychology from York University. His doctoral thesis, *The Competitive Environment: Effects and Influences*, drew on both academic and experiential sources: as a former player in the Philadelphia Flyers organization, and as a hockey coach at York University and in Italy, John is well-versed in the psychology of competition and motivation. His academic interests in statistics and computer modelling led to his work in developing several profiling and selection systems: the Personal Orientation Profile (POP), the Management Potential Profile (MPP), the Career Search Personal Profile (CSPP), and, most recently, the Quality Service Profile (QSP).

As a consultant with the Self Management Group, John has an enviable track record in success coaching for groups that range from professional athletes, teachers, and coaches to senior executives. In a variety of unique programs and seminars, he deals with many aspects of attitude management, effective motivation, and team building. He has also written, and contributed to, a number of books and articles on organizational growth, training, and competition in sports and business.

Bob McHardy, the president of P.L.U.S. Corporation, and a principal of the Self Management Resources Corporation, is an accomplished public speaker, management trainer, sales trainer, and executive coach. Since 1990, Bob has helped build the P.L.U.S. Corporation into a major training organization that works with some of North America's largest banks, trusts, insurance companies, and sales organizations. His popular seminars and training programs, which focus on the distinctive "Managing Effort" approach pioneered by the P.L.U.S. Corporation, have earned him the respect of his colleagues, and made the concept of "self-management" an industry benchmark.

About the Self Management Group

The Self Management Group is a privately held group of companies that provides a comprehensive range of consulting, profiling, development, and training services to successful organizations across North America. SMG products and services are focused on attracting, selecting, and creating successful self-managed individuals and organizations.

SMG offers a wide range of seminars, workshops, and training programs devoted to individual development, coaching, leadership, and executive coaching. Other key SMG products include several proprietary profiling tools, such as the Personal Orientation Profile (POP) and the Self Employment Profile (SEP). These profiles are used by major international clients to identify top performers, to initiate career development, and to identify training needs. SMG is also a leader in developing and maintaining electronic recruiting and selection systems for corporate clients throughout North America.

More information on SMG and its programs and products is available: visit our website at www.self-management.com.

Acknowledgements

This book represents the realization of a longstanding ambition. We dedicate it to all the winners who have helped us understand the power of the self-management process, and we take this opportunity to thank the many people who contributed to its development and its final form.

Thanks first to our colleagues at SMG, who provide a supportive, stimulating environment. The SMG consultants have all helped to refine the principles of self-management that we discuss in this book—and they illustrate those principles every day.

We would also like to acknowledge the thousands of people who have participated in our workshops and seminars over the last two decades. The experiences they have shared with us have helped to clarify our principles, as well as to suggest many practical strategies for self-management.

Finally, thanks to Mitch Cichy for his design skills and creativity, and to On-line Editing for editorial and production services.

Table of Contents .

WINNERS ACT

ON THEIR

OWN

AUTHORITY.

INTRODUCTION

The Self-Management Process

Some people are conspicuously successful. This is never just a matter of luck: success is *planned* and *achieved*, and it is primarily the result of *self-management*. These self-managers consciously apply a process that looks something like this:

SELF-MANAGERS

- DETERMINE THEIR OWN GOALS, OBJECTIVES, AND EXPECTATIONS

- FIGURE OUT WHAT THEY NEED TO DO—THE BEHAVIOR OR ACTIVITY, THE STRATEGY OR GAME PLAN

- MAKE A COMMITMENT TO THE BEHAVIOR OR ACTIVITY

- *KEEP* THE COMMITMENT

- GIVE THEMSELVES CREDIT FOR KEEPING THE COMMITMENT

- EVALUATE THEIR PERFORMANCE OF THE ACTIVITY

- EVALUATE THE RESULTS

- SEEK RESOURCES FOR SELF-IMPROVEMENT AND DEVELOPMENT

- EVALUATE THE OVERALL PROCESS, OVER A PERIOD OF TIME, TO DECIDE WHETHER TO CONTINUE IT, ADJUST IT, OR DISCONTINUE IT

How does this process compare to yours? These activities may all seem straightforward enough—but do you consciously follow all of these steps?

Most people probably do use this sort of approach, at least some of the time, and to some extent—and when they do, they are probably at their best. They are self-managing: they are creating the terms and definitions of their personal and professional success.

SOMETIMES, UNSUCCESSFUL PEOPLE

ARE JUST UNLUCKY.

BUT SUCCESSFUL PEOPLE

ARE NEVER JUST LUCKY.

THEY CREATE THEIR SUCCESS.

This book will help you to take charge of your life, to build on your strengths and your achievements, and become a better self-manager. With an awareness of the process and the principles of self-management, you can address every aspect of your life, developing direct, practical strategies for improvement.

The Challenge

We come into this world as "internal" beings. Our earliest behaviors are internally motivated. We are intrinsically driven to fulfil our own needs—needs for food, sleep, human contact, and stimulation.

So what happens to us? What causes us to gradually become more "external," to look outside ourselves for motivation and direction? Why do we find ourselves pulled between the need to please others and the need to please ourselves? What makes thinking, acting, and choosing for ourselves such a challenge for us? Why is it difficult to make important life decisions, or even simple day-to-day decisions? Why do we so often feel that we are not in control of our lives, that other people can and do pull our strings? Why does what "others will think" have so much effect on our ability to set goals, choose a course of action, or make changes in our lives?

In this book, we intend to address these questions, and to show how you can regain control of your life. By using your innate ability to be internal and to self-manage, you can improve the results you are getting in your life. This means not only less stress and less guilt, but more discipline, more control, more personal power, more confidence, and more success.

The Loss of the "Internal"

Although we all start out as internally driven individuals, we soon learn that other people want us to do certain things—and that they will reward us for the desired behavior and punish us for undesired behavior. This manipulation and control by society, parents, family, friends, teachers, coaches, managers, and colleagues has a conditioning effect on us. Gradually, we learn that others know better, that they will tell us what to do, and that this is an easy system. Internal drives are replaced by external motivations.

WE *KNOW* THAT WE HAVE
THE POWER TO CHOOSE,
BUT WE *LEARN* TO
LET OTHERS CHOOSE.

Throughout our years of growth and development, we are surrounded by a variety of authority figures, who create or modify external circumstances in order to influence or control our behavior. We soon learn that, when we comply, we will be rewarded in many ways, perhaps with affection, attention, encouragement, even money and gifts. We come to associate our actions with positive or negative external consequences, and, over time, we learn that other people will provide us with the motivations and reasons for us to act. We also come to depend on the approval of others, sometimes even the approval of people we hardly know. That approval becomes the index of our accomplishments.

Conditioned in this way to look outside ourselves, we are turned away from our inner drives. The constant association of socially approved actions and external rewards imposes norms of behavior on the child, the student, or the employee. In one sense, that is a good thing—ask any parent, teacher, or employer. The application of external motivations and the imposition of basic, acceptable standards of conduct make it possible for people simply to get along together, for society to work.

No one disputes the need to prepare people to function in society. Socialization is one of the objectives of "education" in its widest sense. Unfortunately, most education, based on systems of external motivations, external controls, and external rewards, takes advantage of the conditioned tendency to seek and accept direction and approval from others. Everything is already in place for this sort of education, and its results are fairly reliable. For example, think of the classic image of a classroom: rows of children sitting quietly, facing the front, seeking approval, checkmarks, and gold stars.

It is considerably more challenging—and riskier—to try to educate people by developing their internal motivations. The noblest goal of education in our society is to create self-directing individuals who respect the necessary constraints of society, yet create their own goals, motivation, and satisfactions. In practice, however, education often falls short of this praiseworthy ambition.

The processes of social conditioning interfere with people's inherent potential to develop genuinely individual, internal motivation. It is easy to stop relying on those sources of self-direction and self-approval, to doubt them or to let them go altogether, when so many older, wiser, and more powerful people are ready to tell us what to do and why we should do it, and then arrange rewards and punishments accordingly. And it is even easier to develop a dependency on those instructions, rationales, and reinforcements. The very structure of the family, the school, and the workplace often requires and rewards a passive acceptance of direction and external control. Even in our adult lives, we find people living out a prolonged "childhood," unable, or, in many cases, unwilling, to advance beyond the early stages of our social conditioning.

Growing Up

The social conditioning that tends to replace internal drives with external motivations is a necessary, but not a sufficient, condition for a full human life. Maturity begins when we regain an inner sense of purpose, reclaim our original self-determination, make our own decisions, and choose to direct our abilities towards our own worthy goals. This maturity is not given; it must be acquired.

BEING MANAGED MEANS

FOLLOWING DIRECTIONS:

SELF-MANAGEMENT MEANS

FINDING THEM.

This book will help you understand the resistance, both within and without yourself, to becoming a self-manager. It will set out the principles of self-management, helping you to understand self-management and to realize your potential to become a better self-manager. We believe this book will help you become a better, more productive parent, teacher, coach, manager or employer, and partner or spouse. Self-management skills will make you more organized, more productive, more satisfied, and more personally fulfilled. All this may sound like a tall order! But what we promise is really no more than the best you can ask of yourself—consistently, on a daily basis.

This book grows out of more than twenty years of consulting to businesses and corporations, and to individuals—the people who run businesses and the people who work in them. Again and again, we have helped managers and executives face their essential challenge: to get results—to motivate employees and workforces to achieve desired objectives. And again and again, we have found that the solution is not to somehow manage people better, or more, or harder. Since you can't *make* people work, adjusting the externals seldom has any real long-term success. What we have found, instead, is that you can train and encourage people to *manage themselves*. When they do, they work harder, they work more productively, and they have more professional and personal fulfillment. They get the results. Everybody wins.

For years, then, we have been stressing the value of *self-management* by helping business managers realize that their main objective is to develop self-managers. But that is a lesson that should be learned by anyone—parent, teacher, coach, or employer—who has the power to influence others, and who is in some way responsible for other peoples' lives, actions, and future. When dealing with our children, students, or employees, we have a choice: we can sustain people's dependency on externals, or we can support their growth and development as self-managers. Anyone in a "position of responsibility" should recognize that the responsibility has crucial *limits*. Responsibility for one's children, for example, includes an effort to transfer that responsibility to *them*. The most "responsible" person, then, is the one who does not attempt to take responsibility for everything. By encouraging children, students, or employees to take up their own responsibilities, good parents, teachers, or managers demonstrate their responsibility—to others and to themselves.

Nine Principles

In this book, we will examine the nine principles of self-management, to help you begin a process of recollection that will strengthen your self-management skills. Self-management is, in one sense, quite natural. We all begin as self-managers, and it may very well be our *recollection* of childhood experiences of internal motivation and fulfillment that leads us to find external motivations and reinforcements "limited" or "hollow." Although many people express such feelings of frustration or dissatisfaction, few perceive their source. It is difficult to focus clearly on the nature and effects of our social conditioning. Although socialization is an elaborate and often arbitrary process, it strikes us as purely "natural," something we simply take for granted.

This unquestioning acceptance must be overcome by a process of *reconditioning*. The point is not, however, to *reject* our socialization and conditioning, but to rediscover internal motivations and the strength of self-determination, and so integrate being managed with self-managing. Self-management is individually liberating, but socially responsible.

The nine principles that follow may be familiar enough as propositions—but we offer them here as challenges:

1. Performance: the key to success
2. Expectations dictate performance
3. Reinforcement creates habits
4. Motivate yourself—others can't
5. Maximize return on energy (ROE)
6. Manage effort
7. Manage self-confidence
8. Commit yourself
9. Decide once: psychological time management

By themselves, on the page, these principles may seem simple enough. We all know, for example, that self-confidence is important; everyone would agree that positive reinforcement encourages behavior. Self-managers, however, don't just *assent* to these principles. They act them out, day by day, in a systematic fashion.

Are self-managers rare? Not really. Everyone is a self-manager, at least some of the time. But few people are self-managers fully, consistently, and systematically. This book is intended to help you identify just when—and more importantly, why—you have been a self-manager. There is a quick way to focus on these episodes: think of the times that you have been happiest, most productive, and most successful. Chances are that those high points were directly related to strong self-management. Now think about how you would do if you performed like that all the time! It's not impossible. If you begin to *recognize* the self-managing strategies and activities that were behind your best successes, you can extend and strengthen them. You will become increasingly conscious of your self-management potential—and the opportunities to use it.

YOU ARE ACCOUNTABLE

FOR YOUR RESULTS,

BUT

YOU ARE RESPONSIBLE

FOR YOUR PERFORMANCE.

PRINCIPLE ONE
PERFORMANCE: THE KEY TO SUCCESS

We Are Measured by Results

Success of any kind depends on getting results. In every aspect of our personal and professional lives, we are measured by the results we achieve, and we tend to measure others in the same way. We are especially aware of this in sports and business, where little allowance is made for circumstances, conditions, or environments. The pressures of competition and the non-negotiable demands of the bottom line force an almost exclusive focus on the results. The hard fact—one that cannot be avoided—is that, in any context, it's the results that count.

We are measured by results. Results are what we focus on, and they are what others focus on. This is human nature. In almost every situation, results are the first thing to be considered. Only after results have been assessed do we consider performance. For instance, ask any athlete, "How did the game go?" The answer that he or she will offer—and the answer that we usually are interested in—is "We won" or "We lost." When the answer is "We lost," performance becomes an issue: "Well, how did you play?" The answer, "We played well," offsets the loss, but does not really compensate for the poor results.

This focus on results is common in every context. Think of the questions you use yourself to find out what is going on: "How much... ," "When... ," "What happened...." Also, think about how you respond to questions about your activities. In most circumstances, results are the beginning and the end of the discussion. Only when the results are perceived to be poor does performance become relevant—and discussions of performance almost always seem to be after-the-fact rationalization.

The habit of judging—and being judged—by results is established early, during our conditioning by parents, teachers, coaches, and other authorities. As part of that conditioning, certain behaviors are associated with certain consequences, either pleasant or unpleasant. We learn to expect positive or negative reinforcement in response to our results. More significantly, we learn that the rewards and punishments depend on the outcome—not on how we feel about the task, whether or not we want to do it, or the attitude with which we do it.

And later, when we evaluate other people, we look for just the same kind of evidence of whether or not their behavior is "satisfactory"—the objective results. We are seldom aware of the process, intentions, or motivations that produce the results— and when we are, we have an extremely limited and unreliable understanding of these things. Often, the only thing that we can observe directly is results. Consequently, when we judge other people's actions, we *keep score*. First we look at the results. Later, we may consider why certain outcomes occurred, but always after the results—and usually only to make exceptions and excuses. After all, we may think, when the results are good, does it really matter why? And judging intentions is complex, time-consuming, and often difficult: the best we can hope for is an educated guess.

In any event, considerations of motive never lead us to overlook the results. We are all too conscious that our methods of identifying or proving internal motivations and purposes are fallible. Motives can be very difficult to express; more dangerously, they are easy to misrepresent. Small wonder that, in the majority of cases, we proceed directly to an evaluation of a person's actions in terms of results, which are objective, directly observable, and easily compared. The world recognizes results.

Results and Performance

We know that results are critical: they are what we work for. The only way to get results is to maximize performance, since it is the performance that leads to results. Often these two terms are used interchangeably. But there is a crucial distinction to be made. Results are indeed directly related to performance: they are the best available evidence of the quality and quantity of a person's performance, and it is on the basis of results that we rate performance. Usually, however, by the time we can weigh the results, the performance itself—a vital, ongoing process—is over, or has gone ahead.

Figure 1.1
Comparison of Performance and Results

Performance	*Results*
➠ *Internal*	➠ *External*
➠ *Process*	➠ *Outcome*
➠ *Success Defined Relative To Potential*	➠ *Success Defined In Terms Of What is Achieved*
➠ *Attitudes and Effort Primary*	➠ *Attitudes and Effort Secondary To Outcome*
➠ *Controllable*	➠ *Can Be Influenced*
➠ *Management By Effort - MBE*	➠ *Management By Objectives - MBO*

As the above figure suggests, performance and results are related as process and outcome, the first essentially internal and unobserved, and the second observable and objectively evaluated. Questions of intention, motive, and effort are irrelevant to the judgment of *results*, but they are crucially relevant to considerations of *performance*. Attempts to lose weight offer a good example of the relation between the two concepts. The *results*—say, a weight loss of five pounds in two weeks—are objective, measurable evidence of a person's success. But the performance required to achieve that success—a matter of effort, commitment, and self-control—simply does not appear in the results.

What Do We Do Well When We Do Well?

The difference between performance and results is more than a question of sequence, or even of cause and effect. Results follow performance, but performance does not wholly determine results. Other factors, often beyond a person's control, intervene, sometimes changing the nature of the results in unexpected or uncontrollable ways. Each person is fully responsible for his or her performance, but seldom, if ever, can a person truly be said to be fully responsible for the results by which he or she is judged. When performance is not clearly distinguished from results, this fact can encourage a kind of fatalism. If results are partially beyond our control, we may say, then in what sense do we have any responsibility for good results or poor results? Could success just be a lucky fluke, or simply the consequence of "doing what we are told to do"? How much credit can we really take for "following the rules"?

These doubts follow naturally from our conditioned dependency on external direction and motivation—and from a related tendency to equate "success" with "results." There are plenty of people ready to tell us what to do, and ready to praise or blame according to how well we measure up to their expectations. An exclusive focus on external motivations and objective results leaves little room for a genuinely personal, individual sense of effort and achievement. Even when we "do well," we may mistake the nature of our success. Properly speaking, "success" is determined internally; it has just as much to do with performance as it does with results.

An accurate analysis of "success" and "failure," then, depends on clearly distinguishing performance from results. Often, it's the people who are under the most pressure to perform well who are most familiar with this sort of distinction. Professional golfers, for instance, know that you just can't control the results: you can pull together years of practice, your sense of the wind, the lay of the fairway, and the balance of the club, to make a perfect *shot*—that still winds up buried in the lip of a bunker. Everything about the performance can be just right, but the results can be just wrong.

YOU ARE *ACCOUNTABLE*

FOR YOUR RESULTS,

BUT

YOU ARE *RESPONSIBLE* FOR

YOUR PERFORMANCE.

Self-managers are distinguished by their highly developed understanding of performance. They have discovered where the genuine responsibility for their actions and achievements lies. We can—indeed, we must—take credit (or accept blame) on the basis of results. The external systems and structures of society—family, school, workplace, etc—will see to that. But genuine success depends on taking responsibility for *performance*. To do so is to begin to become a self-manager, by identifying, developing, and enlarging the role of internal commitment, discipline, motivation, and reward.

Many people seem content to tiptoe through life, accepting direction and seeking reinforcement from others, hoping to make it safely to death. They leave their fate and their success in the hands of others. Self-managers, however, choose to pursue results. They take control—but not of results; nothing is more exhausting, more frustrating, than trying to control the uncontrollable. Rather, they take charge, where they can, of the components of performance: talent, attitude, and opportunity.

The Elements of Performance

Three factors interact to determine performance. The process can be represented as an equation:

Figure 1.2
The Performance Equation

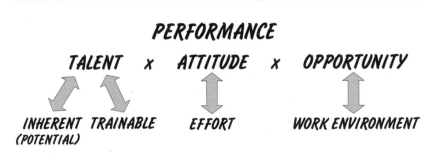

Three primary success factors correspond to three essential attributes: talent, attitude, and opportunity. The three attributes interact to determine performance. The performance "value" of the three factors is produced by multiplication, not by simple addition. Each makes its own distinctive contribution; a very high level of talent, for example, cannot compensate fully for poor attitude. Striking deficiencies in any category don't just lower the final value of performance: they are likely to reduce the value sharply. And if there is a zero score in any category, the calculated value must also be zero, no matter how high the other values may be.

Success Factors

Talent, attitude, and opportunity are all "success factors"—the sorts of things we commonly refer to in trying to explain why and how people achieve good results. "Talent" can refer to a great variety of characteristics, including special skills, experience, and education, as well as less easily defined capabilities: "street smarts," "empathy," or "knowhow." Success is also explained by "attitude," variously qualified as "expectations," "outlook," "determination," "discipline," or "commitment." Successful people have the right abilities and attitudes; they also seek out opportunities to be successful. Sometimes we are inclined to discount "opportunity" as a matter of luck. In fact, opportunities are just as much a matter of selection; they are among the controllable elements of performance. For example, in seeking specific careers, people deliberately choose opportunities in which they can maximize their talent and effort.

Success factors are grounded in personal attributes. That is why we remain responsible for performance, no matter how much of a contribution is made to our actions by external motivations and reinforcements. Distinguishing the elements of performance, rather than focusing on results, clarifies the nature of this responsibility—and shows where we can take control directly, effectively, and productively.

Talent

Two kinds of talent contribute to performance. "Inherent" or "natural" talent refers to a person's *potential*, and remains relatively constant. Inherent talent includes such things as personality, intelligence, sensitivity, empathy, and common sense. Such attributes are evident to most observers, even though they may not be easily documented or tested. Fully developed by the time a person reaches adolescence or early adulthood, inherent talent tends to dictate choices in academic and career contexts. A choice between arts and science, between entrepreneurship and employment, or between sales and service proceeds from, and provides evidence of, inherent talents.

"Trainable" talent, in contrast, is not inherent but acquired, and it can be trained. It includes such things as detailed knowledge about a discipline or subject area, acquaintance with specific procedures and routines, familiarity with established processes, specific skill sets, and other kinds of formal education. Trainable talent is continually developed through observation, education, training, and experience. Thus a person's trainable talent can always be increased, given the appropriate training or learning experiences.

Talent and Responsibility

Some people very easily and naturally take credit for their talents and abilities, even when they admit that there is a difference between the talent they are given and the abilities they acquire. In fact, the capacity to learn and retain knowledge and skills is itself inherent. While no one has control over the inherent talent he or she enjoys, no one else can be said to be responsible for it, or be blamed for any apparent deficiency. However, few people really take full responsibility for the talents they do possess: very few ever realize their full potential.

Responsibility for trainable talent is more complex, since it may be shared with those who identify training needs and provide effective instruction, coaching, and support. For the self-manager, trainable talent may be a shared responsibility. In some cases, when a self-manager sees an opportunity for growth, he or she will seek a coach or mentor. However, the process always *begins* with the individual. As a result of early conditioning, we are often led to renounce our responsibility for this sort of self-development. Many aspects of a traditional upbringing and education are designed to tell people what is best for them, rather than to allow people to independently discover what they do best. As a consequence, most people— even those regarded as successful—have not in fact maximized their potential. In the process, inherent strengths may be neglected, and eventually atrophied, so increasing the individual's reliance on external motivation.

Self-managers, then, make themselves responsible for their knowledge and the development of their skills, but their trainers, companies, or coaches also have a part to play. In our workshops, we'll often ask participants, "Who is responsible for developing your talent?" The answer that generally comes back *sounds* like self-management: "I am." Admirable as this response may be, true self-managers know that others share in this development. Therefore, they seek out training and coaching when and where they need it.

Inherent and trainable talent together make up part of the "can-do" element of performance. Barring a lucky accident, or an extraordinary effort, there is no success without a baseline of inherent talent. Every sports coach knows that, and talent (or potential talent) is usually the first thing that is scouted in new players—or in new employees. Even more important, however, is talent that can be *trained*. Very few people realize their full potential, because they fail to continue to develop their talents. Life is a *continuous* process of development. There is never a point at which you should consider that your learning is complete. Consider the increasing number of retirees who return to school to take graduate and post-graduate degrees. Twenty years ago, the idea of a seventy-year-old MA student seemed odd, even ludicrous—but why? Only because of the unspoken assumption that education was required only by young people, and only as a preparation for thirty or forty years of wage earning.

Effort and Attitude

Talent, both inherent and trainable, is a key determinant of a person's performance. The difference between great potential and great performance, however, is a person's attitude and effort, their habits of thought and their habits of behaviour.

ATTITUDE = HABITS OF THOUGHT

EFFORT = HABITS OF BEHAVIOR

In our workshops, we explore the concepts of attitude and effort and their relationship. Understanding this relationship seems to be critical to developing the skills of self-management. Especially important is the realization that attitude and effort are direct determinants of one another. For example, hard work with little or no positive result can have a detrimental effect on one's attitude: effort without results reduces attitude. And a poor attitude eventually leads to less effort. The resulting frustration and discouragement often lead people to quit trying.

The attitude/effort component of performance, then, is critical. The distinction between attitude and effort, on the one hand, and talent, on the other, is clear in principle, but it is not always observed in practice. We often find it easiest to attribute success to talent, and to neglect the role of both attitude and effort.

ATTITUDE = QUALITY OF ENERGY

EFFORT = QUANTITY OF ENERGY

This can have unfortunate, wasteful consequences: often, performance problems are too narrowly understood as talent issues. When people are simply not making enough of an effort, no amount of skills training, extra courses, or experience will boost performance. A failing student may not need extra tutoring, but extra effort; a poorly performing employee may not lack skills, but self-discipline. Such problems have to do with "will-do," not "can-do." One of the biggest wastes of resources for parents, teachers, and employers is attempting to address "will" issues as though they were "can" issues. Not every performance problem can be solved by more training or more education: if the problem stems from *attitude*, no amount of skills development will help.

The "will-do" component of performance involves both habits of behavior and habits of thought. When we ask people in our workshops "Who is responsible for attitude and effort?" an interesting discussion always takes place. Many will say that it's shared, since it's only natural for other people and the environment to affect attitude and effort. The real question, though, is "Do those external circumstances *have* to influence what you do? Who decides whether they do or not?" The self-manager answers, "Actually, *I* decide whether or not they make a difference—they don't *have* to."

Ultimately, attitude and effort are self-determined. The responsibility for your attitude and effort is entirely yours. Ask yourself the following questions:

- Who tells you how to think about a situation?
- Who determines your reaction to an event?
- Who gets you up in the morning?
- Who tells you how hard to work?

The self-manager answers these questions—and questions like them—with the simple words, "I do!"

A good illustration of responsibility for effort was provided in a recent workshop we conducted for sales representatives. One rep complained that his attitude and effort, and therefore his results, were adversely affected by his manager's style, the commission scale, the competition, and other external factors. He was, in fact, performing poorly. But another rep, who had the same manager, the same commission scale, and the same competition to deal with was performing exceptionally well. In fact, she was leading the company in sales that year. So it was apparent that the difference in performance was due to *internal* rather than external factors.

Each individual is fully and uniquely responsible for this element of performance. Habitual effort levels, sometimes referred to as a "work ethic," tend to be formed early in people's lives. Like all deeply rooted habits, they are hard to change.

PAST PERFORMANCE PREDICTS FUTURE PERFORMANCE—

IF NOTHING CHANGES.

PAST PERFORMANCE *DOES NOT* PREDICT

FUTURE PERFORMANCE

IF *ANYTHING* CHANGES.

SOMETHING ALWAYS CHANGES!

It's commonly said that "past performance predicts future performance"; it is much more accurate, however, to observe that "past effort always predicts future effort," since the habits that determine effort resist change so stubbornly.

PAST EFFORT PREDICTS FUTURE EFFORT.

Circumstances have less to do with effort than one's habits or effort history. For most people, effort levels tend to be consistent. It is challenging to establish good habits of behavior and thought, and it is challenging to reinforce them effectively. Most often, people tend to associate good results with talent, because the connection seems more obvious and direct. Very talented people, however, may achieve good (but never outstanding) results without really working very hard; rewarding their results actually has the effect of conditioning them not to work hard.

Effort and Responsibility

Who is responsible for effort? This simple question is complicated by our conditioning and our common dependence on external motivation. If you ask a teacher, parent, or manager, "Who is responsible for the effort that child or employee makes?", the answer is often, "I am." But if you ask a teacher, parent, or manager, "Who is responsible for *your* effort?", the answer is usually the same—"I am."

Such answers exhibit good intentions, but a potentially damaging confusion between controllables and non-controllables, and between results and performance. A manager, for instance, is certainly *accountable* for the results his or her employees achieve through their efforts, but the manager cannot really be *responsible* for the efforts that other people make. At best, managers control their own efforts, and seek to influence other people's attitudes and effort habits through leadership. Similarly, while parents and teachers have a duty to coach and develop good attitudes and high effort in children, this obligation is not well-served by assuming *responsibility* for the effort, or by attempting to control it directly. The habits that make up the "will-do" component of performance can be changed—but only from within, as the best parents, teachers, coaches, and managers learn.

Old Behaviors Erode New Attitudes

Any attempt to change habits from the outside tends to focus either on attitudes or on behavior—but long-term performance can only be improved if both are changed simultaneously. Many managers know about the "honeymoon glow" that follows every pump-up session, new incentive program, or motivational seminar. But if you change attitudes, and do not change actual behaviors, the old behavior will undermine the new attitudes. These exercises in "attitude management," while they make employees feel good about their work or themselves, seldom establish any productive long-term behavior. It's like old-time revival meetings: plenty of people get "saved," but most of them backslide as soon as the preacher leaves town. A person's attitudes, because they are private, internal, and unexpressed, are not the sort of thing that can be managed— except by the person *himself*.

New Behavior Erodes Old Attitudes

Similarly, attempts to alter effort levels by changing behavior, without any attitudinal change, can have only short-term effects. When new procedures, new activities, or new routines are introduced, the focus is still on externals. The changes occur in the environment, not in the person. There may be a brief "holiday" effect, as the old routines are left behind, but it can't last long. Without deeper attitudinal reforms to support the new behaviors, changing tasks and activities will be ineffective in the long run.

So long as you believe yourself to be responsible for other people's effort, you can only coax them to perform better. Coaxing strategies have little long-term success. Although they are meant to work "from the outside in," they deal exclusively in externals, and never really get "in." When people are being coaxed, they seldom internalize the recommended priorities or values. They merely agree to be directed, in the hope of receiving a reward, or simply so that the coaxing will stop. By contrast, coaching sets the responsibility for effort squarely before the individual. The best coaches avoid working "from the outside in." Instead, they change the ordinary patterns of following instructions and receiving rewards: they focus on performance as well as results, and urge each individual to explore his or her inner sources of motivation. Coaxing is, essentially, a mistaken attempt to share the *effort*; coaching shares the *results*.

Self-managers respond well to coaching; in fact, they seek it out. But they are uncomfortable with coaxing. When they are coaxed, they take it as an imputation that they are not self-managing, not taking responsibility for their attitude and effort. To self-managers, then, coaxing seems to miss the point of what they do.

If you are being coaxed, by a manager, for example, one practical response is to clarify the situation. Take full responsibility for your effort and attitude, and advise your manager that these two elements of performance are now under *your* control. In this way, you can take over the job of motivating yourself, and set out the terms in which you intend to succeed.

Attitude is crucial to performance. And it is equally important to recognize who is responsible for attitude. Often, due to our early conditioning, we make *others* responsible for our attitude. So, for example, an employee may complain, quite sincerely, that he "doesn't feel like working today"— and an employer may feel, equally sincerely, that it is *her* problem, not his. This is unacceptable. Our effort and attitude are 100% controllable—by us. Conditioning, however, tends to obscure this responsibility. Talented people are often reinforced for talent alone, regardless of their efforts. As a result, some very talented people never learn to work hard.

Opportunity and Environment

Good performance depends, then, on the interaction of talent and effort. But it also depends on the right opportunity.

Consistent success is explained by being the right person in the right place, at the right time. Often, opportunity appears to be a matter of good fortune—an accidental arrangement of external circumstances to which a person's strengths and abilities are ideally suited. And perhaps the most appealing "success" stories are those that stress this fortuitous element—it's pleasant to imagine that success can sometimes be achieved with little effort, even with little talent. But opportunities are not purely accidental. They arise naturally in our experience as a product of choices that we have made.

Opportunity and Responsibility

At some very general levels of description, no one can be said to choose the "world" they inhabit. We have no say in the time or place of our birth, the circumstances and nature of our early development. But, from a very early stage, we do exercise a considerable degree of freedom in selecting smaller, more precisely defined contexts—and the range of opportunities they offer. These choices are often influenced by considerations of our talents, or the effort we are willing to make. But to some degree, the choice remains a personal one, and we each bear a degree of responsibility for such selections.

Opportunity, then, cannot be discounted as a purely external, uncontrollable element of performance. It's worth noting that we are quick to blame people for failing to take advantage of opportunities—not just any opportunities, of course, but opportunities that are well-suited to their abilities, and which have arisen naturally as a result of choices they have made. If we hold other people responsible for failing to take opportunities, we should apply the same standard to ourselves. That is, we should consider ourselves responsible for the opportunities that present themselves to us, and that we create in making our choices.

It is tempting, especially when we are not pleased with our performance, to blame poor results on poor luck. But the same opportunities exist for all of us, although inherent differences may make us more or less willing, able, and ready to take them. A "victim mentality" argues that such differences *deprive* people of opportunities. This perspective, however, considers only the possibilities that are excluded. There may be opportunities that are not right for us—but there are also the opportunities, large and small, that we *have* taken.

DON'T COMPLAIN ABOUT THE TEMPERATURE WHEN YOU CONTROL THE THERMOSTAT.

Even those who are unhappy with their circumstances should recognize that their discontent has to with the conditions they have *accepted*, not with the withholding of some preferable alternative.

Environment and Responsibility

Opportunities are at least partially within our control, and within the range of our choices. We actively seek out opportunities, and we have even more responsibility for the ways in which we respond to them, alter them, and create an environment within them. Even within the constraints of an opportunity that is apparently forced on us (school, family relationships), we have some liberty to react and to act upon the circumstances. We must believe ourselves responsible, not only for recognizing and taking advantage of an opportunity, but for creating or modifying its environment. Conditioning often makes this difficult. It is easy, for instance, to assume that the "atmosphere" of a home, a classroom, or a workplace is just "natural," or else is the work of others. In fact, environments are *constructed*, and require active participation, support, and modification.

Here too, then, a self-manager takes responsibility, contributing to an environment, rather than passively accepting it. Consider, for instance, the way top-performing athletes can transform a team. Rather than allowing a team environment to influence his performance, a Gretzky or a Jordan raises the team to his level. In business, the best achievers are those who do not allow workplace standards to set their performance levels—and they are also the best employees, since their achievements constantly "raise the bar" for their colleagues. They *create* an environment, raising the level of morale, increasing standards for activity and productivity, and developing an atmosphere that works well for everyone.

Putting It All Together

Good performance depends on having all three performance elements in place: talent, effort, and opportunity. When any one element is lacking, the performance equation will inevitably yield a poor result. We often have great expectations of a match between high levels of talent and a great opportunity—but if the effort is not there, we are likely to be disappointed. A talented athlete, for example, drafted for the majors, may have great skills and an opportunity every amateur dreams of. But if the player doesn't prepare for the professional league, or doesn't work hard, he will soon find himself sidelined.

IF YOU THINK YOU CAN—

OR THINK YOU CAN'T—

YOU'RE RIGHT.

PRINCIPLE TWO
EXPECTATIONS DICTATE PERFORMANCE

Setting Your Own Limits

Self-management begins when you recognize and take respon-sibility for all the elements of your performance. It begins when you decide to pursue results, through the methods and activities that *you* select, rather than rely on others to push you towards methods and results that *they* have chosen. It is necessary to understand the nature of performance, so as to grasp the parameters in which a self-manager acts. Separating performance from results helps identify just what self-managers manage.

Self-management depends on discovering what you can do, as well as what you can't do. It depends on discovering your true potential, and then maximizing it—often breaking through the artificial barriers that can restrict performance and achievement. Very few people ever reach their real limits—that is, their full potential. Often, they stop short at the limits offered, or even imposed, by others.

Self-managers learn how to set their own expectations for effort and results. They use any standards, quotas, or objectives offered by managers, teachers, or employers as guidelines, as indicators of *average* performance levels, not as rules to be followed. They know that expectations, when offered or imposed by others, can operate to their disadvantage, especially when those expectations set limits to what they can achieve. It is easy to "buy into" other people's expectations. But when the "quota" for average performance becomes your own expectation for yourself, you have placed a crucial restriction on your success. Aspiring to the average is really no ambition at all.

Self-managers know that external motivations and reinforcements, typically based on results, usually require less than they are capable of, both in terms of effort and ability. Or, perhaps more importantly, they *sustain* this awareness: plenty of people are aware, in a hazy way, that their rewards are often disproportionate to their efforts. But this knowledge is easy to suppress, and it is much more pleasant to accept other people's positive evaluations at face value. As a result, attaining the average comes to be treated like an accomplishment, when it is really nothing but the avoidance of failure. Self-managers refuse these cheap satisfactions. They know that the generally accepted limits to performance do not necessarily apply to them: they set their own limits.

The Power of Expectations

Expectations set the effective limits to performance.

EXPECTATIONS DICTATE PERFORMANCE.

This is perhaps the most powerful principle of psychology. And it works, time and time again. We see this principle working around us all the time; it occurs in every human context, at every level. The setting of expectations is a function of three interrelated aspects:
- what we expect of ourselves
- what we expect of others
- what others expect of us

In each case, expectations are generally realized. There are two reasons for this. First, we do, as a rule, tend to form fairly accurate expectations of what is going to happen. A significant proportion of our existence depends on barely conscious assumptions, beliefs, and expectations that are regularly and consistently satisfied by experience. But the close fit between expectations and events also has to do with the way in which expectations condition just what we perceive and experience. Because we rely on expectations—as a guide to the next moment, the next day, and the rest of our lives—we tend to look for just the events, actions, behaviors, and situations that support and validate our expectations. Expectations make our perceptions *selective*, focusing our attention on certain things and excluding many others as simply irrelevant.

The Workings of Expectations

Stereotypes

The complex operation of expectations is evident, for example, in stereotyping. In stereotyping, what we expect of others (and, in some cases, what others expect of us) very strongly determines what is perceived or experienced. Stereotypes create expectations, so much so that anything that does not conform to the stereotype tends to be invisible. There are plenty of examples. Accountants, for instance, are commonly considered to be quiet, introverted people who carry extra sets of batteries for their calculators. Used-car sales reps, according to the stereotype, are hearty, loud, and fast-talking.

Familiar stereotypes like these are virtually ineradicable, since they predispose people to see only the evidence that confirms the stereotype or persuade people to set aside any evidence that contradicts the stereotype. It's worth noting that most people make an exception for their own insurance broker, or for the one professional athlete they met at a PTA meeting, or for the car dealer they buy from. Exceptions like this reflect an awareness that what we actually experience may go beyond the limits of the stereotype—but at the same time, as exceptions, they reinforce the stereotype.

Self-Managers Create Expectations

Self-managers are aware of stereotypes and, more generally, the power of expectations. We cannot live without expectations, and, at some level, we probably cannot do without stereotypes. Self-managers, however, as part of a general awareness of their abilities and potential, recognize stereotyping, and more importantly, refuse its limitations, if it begins to encroach upon their initiatives. Self-managers also *create* their own public image. They use "self-marketing" techniques to create favorable expectations, and to let others know what they can do and when they will do it. (Some of these techniques are discussed later, in Chapter Seven.) In this way, *they* prescribe the expectations by which they will be judged. The general rule—that expectations dictate performance—always holds true. But self-managers ensure that, as much as possible, it is their *own* expectations that shape and set the boundaries to their goals and efforts.

Labels

Labelling also functions, like stereotyping, to create expectations that are satisfied both because they are accurate (to some extent) and because they focus our attention on the behavior we expect to observe in (or are prepared to accept from) the bearers of the labels. Companies, for instance, may enjoy the benefits of labelling. IBM—"Big Blue"—and Bell Telephone— "Ma Bell"—both elicit a generally positive response that is not directly related to any of the organizations' corporate policies or business actions. As a result, a great deal of advertising is devoted to labelling products and organizations. Smaller groups can also cash in on the power of a label: in the days of the "Broad Street Bullies," the Philadelphia Flyers were often ahead in a game before it even started. Good coaches often create a reputation for their team and their players, to take advantage of the power of expectations.

Every label, from a socially conferred title (Honourable Member, Executive Vice-President, Reverend Doctor) to a work-place nickname (Honest John, Steady Eddie, Water-Cooler Willy), creates expectations and directs attention to the actions and behavior that support the label. Like stereotyping, labelling tends to reinforce itself. As a consequence, a senator, president, or member of parliament can carry a load of accusations, imputations, and lawsuits that would sink an ordinary person— simply by virtue of the label. And, like stereotyping, labelling is widespread, often unobserved, and not necessarily objection-able. The expectations that dictate performance have many sources and take many forms.

For self-managers, however, labelling becomes an issue when it is an imposed limitation that restricts their potential or locks them into a cycle of predictable repetition. Once tagged as the "class clown," for instance, a student is seldom expected to get more than a laugh. Unfortunately, such a student may live up to that meagre expectation for the rest of his life.

Reputations

Reputations also create expectations. People who have a reputation for meeting tight deadlines, for example, are often given the tasks with the tightest deadlines—and usually meet them. Like a label, a reputation tends to focus attention on the evidence that confirms the expectations. When the reputation is a good one, of course, this is highly desirable! But when a person's reputation is a bad one, it can be very difficult to overcome others' selective perceptions. Many experienced teachers, for instance, have discovered that a "problem" child's greatest difficulty is having been identified by the system as a "problem." In almost any large institution or organization a reputation can be established very quickly—and will be sustained even when it is later contradicted by actions and behavior.

Expectations and Performance

Stereotyping, labelling, and reputations are all good examples of the way certain kinds of performance are projected and, to some extent, regulated. However, the expectations that really determine how you perform are *your own* expectations. Self-managers know this. Rather than allow other people—or chance circumstances—to define them, they *create* expectations, for others and for themselves. Remember, if you think you can—or if you think you can't—you're right. But what makes you think so—where do your expectations come from?

We usually think expectations are things that *other people* have: teachers establish standards for us, or employers provide quotas, or friends and family make demands on us. All these people have expectations about what we should do. But this is merely a manner of speaking: it means that we respond thoughtfully and deliberately to others' requirements or desires as we set our own expectations. In the final analysis, it is *our* belief in our own goals that allows us to push through adversity and accomplish what we set out to do. Persistent effort comes from within, as an attempt to live up to what *we* have selected as essential, desirable, or valuable.

At worst, the attribution of our own expectations to others suggests that we have not recognized—or that we are trying to refuse—our responsibility to set expectations. Often, what we expect of ourselves does come from outside. But in the course of socialization and early conditioning, we internalize parents', teachers', and peers' expectations, making them our own. We may buy into the stereotypes, for example, or the labels and reputations, that others attribute to us. Or we may internalize a set of academic standards, or a "code" of business practices. Sometimes the labels are positive, the reputations good, the standards and codes worthy. That makes it easier to get along in life—but a little harder to start self-managing. For as long as we think of others as providing or controlling expectations for our performance, our successes can only be measured in *their* terms. Typically, this involves a sacrifice of individual potential. In more extreme cases, the imposition and acceptance of rigid, highly selective expectations effectively substitutes an objective "third person" for the subjective "first person." An individual may come to see, or value, himself or herself only in terms of a function, a role, or a position.

Self-Management and Self-Talk

It is not enough to recognize our responsibility for performance: we need to take control of performance. Our own expectations fix the limits of what we are able to do, in this way determining both the nature and the level of performance. We change expectations—of what we can do, and of how others will perceive us—so as to create room in which to do more and better. We also change and increase expectations so that we can do *other* things, and realize as-yet untapped potential. Adjusting our expectations makes it possible to maximize motivation and drive: when we take on new challenges, we can find new energy.

"Self-talk" is an important element in resetting expectations, but expectations cannot be changed by talk alone. Telling yourself—and telling others—that you have what it takes to reach a given goal is a good first step. *Stating* the terms in which you intend to succeed is one way to take advantage of the power of expectations: it focuses attention on the behavior that will show you to have succeeded. However, self-talk, as a matter of words, is only a beginning. It is a unidimensional stage in the multidimensional process of self-management.

Resetting Expectations: The Ideal Motivational Gap

You *know* you have the ability to reach a goal when your performance achieves the objective. One of the most direct and productive ways to influence performance is to increase expectations, and so too the expectations others have of us. The change must be both of degree and of kind.

Dissonance Theory

The goal of resetting expectations is to create an ideal "incentive gap." As the figure below indicates, the ideal gap between performance and expectation is approximately 25 per cent.

Figure 2.1
Dissonance Theory: Ideal Gap

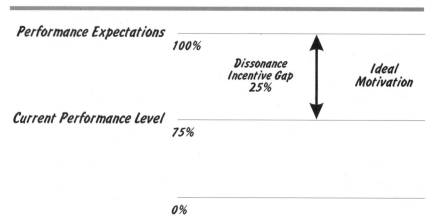

It does not matter who or what sets the expectations for current and desired performance: a larger gap than 25 per cent necessarily provides less motivation, since it will seem too great to overcome (see Figure 2.2).

Figure 2.2
Dissonance Theory: Unrealistic Gap

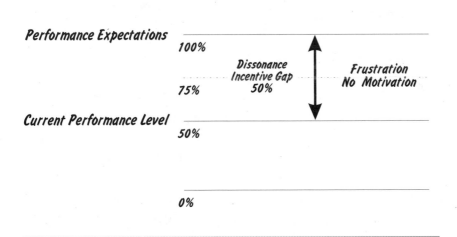

When the gap is too wide, progress seems slow or even nonexistent, and the goal too far away. Frustration and discouragement easily follow. A smaller variation, on the other hand, since it promises correspondingly smaller rewards or reinforcement, will not seem worth the effort (see Figure 2.3).

The ideal gap—about a 25% variation—is typical of a "challenging" objective (see Figure 2.1). Any less, and the task seems "trivial"; any more, and it seems too "tough." We can all rise to a challenge, but few people will even begin to take on a "tough" project—it will probably be just too hard. Like all of us, then, self-managers respond to challenges—but they don't just wait for them to happen: they *create* them.

Figure 2.3
Dissonance Theory: Demotivating Gap

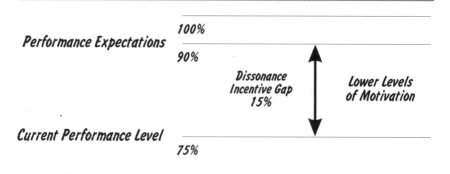

Everyone is motivated to close the ideal incentive gap: they want the 25 per cent. But there are two ways to get it: *lowering* expectations, so that they coincide with current performance, or *increasing* performance, to meet higher expectations. The first way is a lot easier—and it is not really uncommon. People often accept less than they are capable of, less than they deserve, and defend this as "being realistic." "I used to want it all; then I grew up and lost my illusions," they say, making an adult virtue of what they have mistaken for necessity.

Closing the gap by pulling expectations downwards is, in fact, more expedient. It is very difficult, and perhaps impossible, to boost performance by 25 per cent, all at once. Raising expectations requires more than a resolution; it requires a process, with its own specific objects and strategies. The first practical strategy is, of course, to take small steps towards the 25% increase. A small increase in performance tends to raise expectations naturally and to a feasible extent. It's well-known that success breeds success; more remarkable, however, is the way a success creates the very conditions in which it can be surpassed. Every success is the benchmark for a new challenge—an incremental raising of expectations.

Figure 2.4
Continuous Evolution of Performance and Expectations

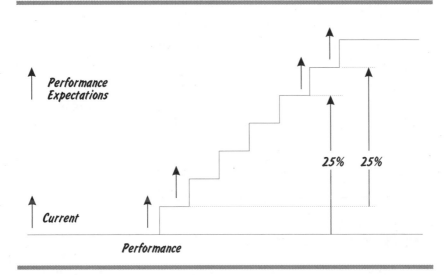

This is well-illustrated by the famous ring toss experiment, which observed subjects' strategies in playing a simple ring toss game. Two groups, preselected as under- and overachievers, were invited to learn how to toss a ring over a peg; no rules at all were imposed. The achievers, typically, began by standing close to the target, making sure that they could succeed with their very first and all subsequent throws. Achievers like to achieve: they create circumstances in which success is likely. But achievers also like a challenge: once they could hit the target easily, they would begin to move back—and then sometimes closer again—to balance increased difficulty against practised success. The underachievers, by contrast, typically started so far away from the target that they could hardly hope to succeed. The gap between what they could do and what they were required to do was simply too great. The high-performing ring toss players, then, by creating conditions for success from the very outset, and by incrementally increasing their expectations, *managed* the incentive gap to their own advantage.

Strategies for increasing performance and expectations follow from a clear and realistic analysis of the three essential components of performance: talent, effort, and opportunity. Expectations mould all three: our performance is the product of current talents, actual effort levels, and management of the opportunities available. All three are open to self-analysis, re-evaluation, and adjustment. By changing, increasing, or improving any of these three components, we can increase our performance expectations. From day to day, we can continually adjust expectations to maintain the ideal 25% incentive gap.

Breaking through Barriers

First, however, we must realize that expectations are indeed ours to determine. The standards, quotas, or objectives that others set for us are based on their necessarily approximate estimates of what we can do, how hard we can work, or on company or industry averages. In most cases, *averages perpetuate averages*: the goals that other people set for us often function as barriers. For years, it was a well-established fact that no human being could run the mile in less than four minutes. Since 1954, however, when Roger Bannister made his record-breaking run, many people have done it. Breaking through such barriers is typically an achievement of self-management: rather than accept given norms as the limits to effort, self-managers take control of the process, maximizing their performance, and aiming for what they believe themselves able to do—which often exceeds what others expect.

So long as we passively accept externally determined expectations, we are unlikely to reach our full potential—or even to *imagine* what it may be. Every parent or teacher knows that it can be difficult to motivate children to better performance. The difficulty, however, is not always due to some sort of resistance in the child: performance-boosting strategies depend on an accurate appraisal of a person's talent, effort, and opportunity. And these internal aspects of a person cannot be directly observed. A talented coach, for instance, doesn't just urge a player to play harder: he or she facilitates the setting of expectations on the basis of a realistic analysis of a player's potential. Without accurate analysis, coaching can under- or overestimate potential—and, as a result, either limit performance or frustrate the individual or team. In both cases, emotional hype tends to replace practical suggestions. (As a consequence, a great deal of "motivational" writing and lecturing in the business world suffers from a tendency to offer encouragement without practical strategies, and recommendations that have no specific, individual foundations.)

Do It Yourself

Talented coaches, experienced parents, and skilled teachers can do much to help you evaluate and establish expectations for your performance. But the person who is in the best position to analyze your abilities, commitment, and opportunities is, of course, yourself. Expectations, as the definite, specific link between what could happen and what does happen—or what is perceived to happen—can be controlled. As such, they are among the materials that self-managers *manage*. Self-managers are typically high achievers because, first, they develop their self-knowledge, and second, they apply it in resetting expectations for themselves—both their own expectations, and those of others.

Expectations, like effort levels and attitudinal levels, can be revised *directly*. Inherent talents tend to remain stable, but labels can be changed, reputations reworked, and stereotypes exploded. To this extent, managing expectations is like marketing yourself: if you can keep your balance, you bill yourself as an acrobat; if you tend to fall down, you put on a clown suit. A juggler who keeps on dropping the balls doesn't have to leave the circus: he just has to change his act. Setting expectations—perhaps in opposition to those others supply, on the basis of an unrealistic appraisal or imposed limits—can *immediately* create new possibilities for successful performance.

Self-managers continually adjust expectations to increase their performance and to grow, both personally and professionally. Taking back control of expectations is an essential element of internal motivation. Under one's own control, expectations can be continuously modified to encourage sustained growth. And since no one knows your current limits better than you do, no one is in a better position to set new levels for performance expectations that can be attained, and then increased. Others may miss the mark; with the best of intentions, they may set expectations so high that they no longer function as a motivation, but as a disincentive. When the difference between what you are expected to do and what you presently do is too great, you may not even try, since the best you can do is "tie or lose." By contrast, when you set an expectation for yourself that you believe represents a significant improvement, you are likely both to try and to succeed—and, with the reinforcement of that success, to reset your expectations again. Each individual success constitutes a step in the continuous process of self-management.

Believe in Yourself

Self-expectancy represents a powerful belief in oneself. The importance of this belief was recognized in Proverbs—"As he thinketh in his heart, so is he"—and more recently in Norman Vincent Peale's *The Power of Positive Thinking*. Peale's first chapter is titled, simply, "Believe in Yourself." This belief has to be more than just self-talk: it depends not only on saying what you will do but on trusting that you can do it—a knowledge that has its evidence in performance. Self-managers build themselves and their lives on the powerful expectation that they can and will succeed. Of course, expectations alone have no power to achieve results. You need expectations, but expectations also need you—to do the thinking, the planning, and the work to realize them. The expectation of success or achievement, however, supports your efforts, keeps you working, helps you keep trying, even in the face of obstacles and setbacks. As the performance equation illustrates, persistent effort is a crucial element of success; positive self-expectations are the most powerful and direct source of this persistence.

Self-managers continually set higher expectations for themselves, and their self-awareness ensures that their goals remain attainable. As a result, they enjoy the satisfaction of accomplishment, and bring even more self-confidence to setting and pursuing new goals. They expect to succeed, and arrange things so that they do; then they add to the challenges. In this way, self-managers promote self-development by continuously increasing the level of expectations. This process can carry on indefinitely. Self-managers don't resolve to be "the best." That is the all-or-nothing, impracticable resolve of those who recognize only their deficiencies. Rather, self-managers, who recognize their strengths as well as their limitations, continue to manage performance and *become better*.

YOU ONLY HAVE TO DO IT UNTIL YOU

WANT TO DO IT;

THEN YOU DON'T HAVE TO DO IT ANY

MORE.

PRINCIPLE THREE
REINFORCEMENT CREATES HABITS

Principles of Reinforcement

Everyone is familiar with the three general principles of reinforcement:

1. Behavior that is positively reinforced tends to be repeated.

This holds true for all types of behavior and attitude. Positive reinforcement is a "reward"; it endorses the behavior, strengthens it, and in time, the behavior becomes a habit. Reinforcements vary from situation to situation and person to person. They are effective in increasing repetition if they are perceived as positive. The development of habitual behavior requires direct, perceived positive reinforcement.

2. If behavior is not positively reinforced, it will tend to be extinguished.

When no positive outcomes are perceived, a behavior is unlikely to be repeated. Here too, the operation of reinforcement depends on how outcomes are *perceived*. A person who goes on a diet, but sees no immediate weight loss, is easily inclined to give up, even though his or her physical condition may have improved in less obvious ways. If behaviors are not perceived to be reinforced, they will disappear.

3. Behavior that is negatively reinforced tends to be extinguished more quickly.

When punishments or negative consequences are associated with a certain behavior, it disappears quickly.

These principles of reinforcement are a part of everyday life. We use reinforcement constantly—and we are also constantly on the receiving end. The operation of reinforcement is central to the formation of habits, to conditioning, and to learning.

Developing Habits through Reinforcement

It is worth stressing the point that desired behaviors or attitudes can only be developed by positive reinforcement. This seems an obvious point, the sort of thing we all know. But, like many of the things we all know, it is often ignored in practice. It's easy to think of examples—the parents who try to improve children's behavior by punishing them for infractions, the teachers who try to improve students' performance by forbidding them extracurricular activities, and so on. A confusion between *extinguishing* undesirable behavior and *encouraging* desirable behavior lies deep in our society's structures and institutions.

If positively reinforced long enough and often enough, behavior becomes habitual. Negative reinforcement and simple non-reinforcement (withholding approval or rewards) can extinguish or diminish the recurrence of unacceptable or unwanted behavior, but they cannot, by themselves, form any new habits of acceptable behavior. Habits are developed through a combination of approaches: old habits must be extinguished, through negative reinforcement, but at the same time, new habits must be encouraged, through positive reinforcement. Ideally, when a choice is possible, new habits are formed by building a positive that replaces (or conflicts with) the negative. Relying on just one or the other side of the process tends to produce only short-term effects. Quitting smoking, for instance, requires more than simply stopping. Stopping is negatively reinforced: you feel worse than you did when you were smoking. But if a competing habit—exercise, for example—is positively reinforced, a whole new non-smoking behavior pattern can establish itself.

What Not to Do vs What to Do

Positive reinforcement is a more powerful principle for developing and growing than negative reinforcement. We are often told that we learn from our mistakes, but all we learn, really, is not to make those mistakes again—if we are lucky. People *often* don't seem to learn from their mistakes at all. When we do learn from our mistakes—when we learn from what we don't do well—we become conscious of only half of our potential. We have conscious incompetence, but we still don't really know what we *can* do, or what we are *good* at.

Figure 3.1
The Four Learning Systems

Learning System	Description	Learning Potential	Label
I			
Conscious Competence	Learning from what we do well.	Full	Self-confident
Conscious Incompetence	Learning from what we don't do well.		
II			
Conscious Competence Unconscious Incompetence	Learning only from what we do well.	1/2	Arrogant
III			
Unconscious Competence Conscious Incompetence	Learning solely from what we don't do well.	1/2	Self-doubting
IV			
Unconscious	No learning.		

We can also learn from what we do well—and evidence suggests that we learn more and better this way. The consequences of success, whether they have to do with congratulations and rewards offered by others, or with an inner sense of accomplishment and completion, are strong reinforcements. Even so, if we learn solely from what we do well, we still miss out on the full potential: we have conscious competence, but not necessarily any conscious incompetence. It's vital to know your strengths, but it's important to know your growth opportunities too. Full learning potential depends on identifying both what we do well and what areas we need to develop. The genuine goal of any educative process, then, should be conscious competence *and* conscious incompetence.

If you suspect you may be in the unconscious competence/conscious incompetence category, you may want to analyze how the people around you have been reinforcing your position. Are you a "self-doubter"? Self-doubters typically downplay their strengths, but they readily acknowledge or emphasize their weaknesses. They make insecure statements, such as "I could never do that," or "I'm too stupid"; the people around them respond, fairly predictably, "Oh yes you could," or "No, you're smart." These responses reward the self-deprecating or insecure statement. If you tend to make self-doubting statements, there is a good chance that the people around you are reinforcing this negative behavior. And if this has been going on for some time, you may have developed a *habit* of making non-confident or self-deprecating statements. (Once you recognize this pattern, however, you can use simple, direct strategies to change your situation. Chapter Seven describes some of these strategies in detail.)

External and Internal Reinforcement

There are two types of reinforcement: external and internal. External reinforcement, both positive and negative, is a familiar part of our socialization, and a major aspect of our upbringing. We quickly become accustomed to the desirable outcomes that result from "approved" behavior. This conditioning has a number of significant consequences. First, the more that is done for us, the less we learn to do for ourselves. The more we look to others for recognition or approval, the less we are likely to supply our own approval. As a result, we become increasingly subject to the influence, and even the control, of others. *They* supply the reinforcements, usually on their own self-interested terms, and *we* move away from our natural self-managing tendencies. The effectiveness of external reinforcement depends on putting someone else in authority over you—and that is the real danger. It's tantamount to saying, "You are the expert: what you think is of more importance than what I think." We all know that there are people whose main motive seems to be to please others. This is commonly seen as a desirable characteristic—but it may very well be deeply connected to an internal deficiency.

External reinforcement is so pervasive and "natural" a feature of our lives that it may seem difficult to question. To what degree, however, can a person take charge of the amount and kind of reinforcement applied in his or her day-to-day life? To what extent can a person become aware of the external reinforcements—comments, events, pressures—that impact his or her daily life? And how can we learn to benefit from the many forms of external reinforcement, yet avoid becoming dependent upon others, or even controlled or manipulated by others?

Self-Reinforcement

The answers to these questions all depend on the concept of *self-reinforcement*. In the process of socialization, every person is intended to internalize the standards and codes supplied by parents, teachers, and other authorities. A parent, for instance, begins by controlling every aspect of a child's existence, but the long-term goal of the parent's work is to bring that sort of supervision to an end, by helping the child develop into a responsible, self-directing person. Mature individuals are expected to take over the role of direction for themselves—and also to take on the role of *approval*.

Self-approval is a key function of the self-manager. Often, however, it is difficult to practise. Conditioning is generally very successful in creating habits of acceptable behavior by supplying external reinforcements. People easily internalize the recommended code of conduct, but not the reinforcement structure. They wind up tending to behave in the approved ways, but still continue to rely on external sources of approval. Not everyone moves to a level of maturity at which direct, active reinforcement by parents, teachers, managers, and other representatives of a society's values and practices is no longer required.

Figure 3.2
Ideal Proportions of Internal and External Reinforcement

Internal	External
✓ Process	✓ Result
✓ Qualitative	✓ Quantitative
✓ Direct	✓ Indirect
90%	**10%**

A key component of self-management is an awareness of the *inner* dimension of reinforcement. The alternative—which is fairly common—is to think of all reinforcement as coming from outside. After all, the examples of reinforcement that come to mind most easily—rewards for passing or for high grades, a manager's praise for an employee, or a bonus, the "attaboys" and "way-to-gos," and so on—all depict "reinforcement" as external. This external reinforcement is grounded in the existence of a hierarchy (the praise and punishments flow downhill) and in the assumption that people in higher positions of authority are better able to make accurate judgments of others' behavior.

Ideal Models of Reinforcement

At any given moment, internal and external reinforcements can be more or less consistent and congruent. In an ideal situation, external reinforcement, whether it is supplied by authority

Figure 3.3
Ideal Reinforcement System

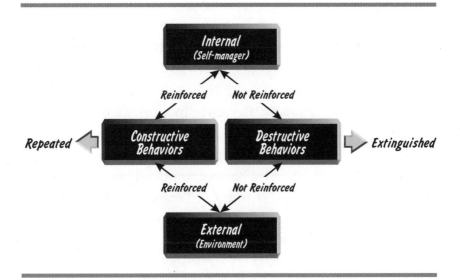

figures, peers, or "society" in general, is consistent with a person's internal reinforcement structure. When the world reinforces the same things the individual self-reinforces, behavior is strengthened, and has a better chance of becoming an enduring habit.

Consider, for example, an athlete who works on a new skill—say, a tennis player practising her serve. When internal reinforcement—feeling more competent—is matched by external reinforcement—more aces, positive comments from her coach, etc—the new behavior (practising) and the new attitude (about practising) will become habitual. Similarly, a person who goes on a weight-loss program, starts to feel better (an internal reinforcement), and finds that friends share his own opinion that he looks better, will be encouraged by the consistency of external and internal reinforcement to continue dieting and exercising.

Confused Models of Reinforcement

When internal and external reinforcements are inconsistent or even contradictory, what is being reinforced can become confused. Such situations create tension or stress, since early conditioning leads us to find disagreement between external reinforcements and internal reinforcements uncomfortable.

"Confused" reinforcements may also undermine habits. The tennis player who, despite hours of work on her serve, still double faults regularly may give up working on her serve, even though internal reinforcements are strong. The dieter who, although he feels better and thinks he looks better, doesn't find that anyone else has even noticed his achievement, may be persuaded, if he is not a self-manager, to give up his weight-loss program. Both of these examples reflect important features of our conditioning. In these cases, an external response, predicated on *results*, overcomes an internal response based on a *process*. We are inclined to give priority to external reinforcement, often neglecting the fact that the world can only reinforce results.

Figure 3.4
Confused Models

---

1. Internal Environment

Way to Go!
(Self-reinforcement)

Excellent Effort   Average Effort   Poor Effort

2. External Environment

Praise/Feedback

Excellent Effort   Average Effort   Poor Effort

Strategies for Confused Models

The relationship between internal and external reinforcements varies from moment to moment, and from context to context. There are four primary strategies for "confused" reinforcement situations:

1. Adjust the internal, based on the external.
2. Change the internal to match the external.
3. Change the external to match the internal.
4. Maintain the internal.

Generally, people seek coherence, hoping to maximize the agreements of internal and external reinforcement, and minimize uncomfortable tensions or clashes. This requires decision-making: the most appropriate reinforcement must be determined, and adjustments to the reinforcement structure must be made accordingly. There are a number of ways to do this, but the method that often seems the most "natural" is to *change* the internal to match the external, or to *repress* the internal in favor of the external. That is what we learn to do during our upbringing, and it is an important element of becoming mature. So, for example, a dieter will deliberately discount or devalue the satisfactions offered by a rich dessert; the strong internal reinforcement is set aside, in an effort to create and sustain new behavior and, eventually, new habits.

However, there are other options. One is simply to maintain the internal, despite its inconsistency with the external. Self-managers typically take this approach, by recognizing the important differences between internal and external reinforcement. Self-managers realize that using external reinforcements to set internal reinforcements may not really resolve the tension. After all, external reinforcements do not "measure up" to internal reinforcements: they differ in kind as well as degree. As suggested above, external reinforcement is predicated on results—the only thing that others can observe and evaluate, and the evaluations are necessarily quantitative.

Internal reinforcement bears on performance, the quality of which is directly perceived only from within, by the individual, whose self-evaluation can be qualitative.

When these distinctions are made, it easy to see how and why a considerable divergence between internal and external reinforcements can be tolerated. In fact, it is quite common: we all know people, for example, who love golf, and who play (and practise) regularly, in the hopes of becoming as good as they can be. Those who are genuinely devoted to the sport strive to attain individual excellence—even when other people, and their own self-evaluations, indicate that they are not very good players. The internal reinforcements of satisfaction and a sense of improvement easily overcome any negative external judgments.

The self-manager's long-term strategy, however, is not merely to sustain internal reinforcements, but to change the external to match the internal. Over the long run, the self-manager's improved performance will get the results that others can see, approve, and reward, and external reinforcement will become commensurate with internal reinforcement.

In a "confused" model, then, a conflict between external and internal reinforcement cannot be resolved simply by calculation; the one cannot really "outweigh" the other. Resolution depends on—and is often revealed by—making a clear distinction between the different modalities of external and internal reinforcement. As mentioned above, we are often conditioned to set aside internal reinforcement in favor of external reinforcement. More self-understanding—and self-management potential—is available, however, if we recognize the way in which apparent differences of reinforcements actually reflect the different natures of external and internal reinforcement.

Self-Management and Self-Reinforcement

Self-management typically involves a reconditioning, an undoing of dependencies created by socialization. Self-management is an evolutionary process. The self-manager continually develops self-reinforcing strategies, learning from external reinforcement, and adjusting internal reinforcement where appropriate. In preceding chapters, we have discussed the importance of distinguishing performance from results, of recognizing our individual responsibility for performance, and reclaiming our internal motivation. We need the same sort of self-knowledge about reinforcement. Self-managers learn to assess the relationship between external and internal reinforcement as more or less complementary. The quantitative, results-based reinforcements provided by peers, employers, and various authorities are seen to be more or less well-adjusted to one's own qualitative, performance-based reinforcements. In this sort of analysis, external reinforcements are "tested" by reference to internal reinforcements, and vice versa—neither is made "the" rule.

For the self-manager, the customary priority of the external is offset—but not displaced—by the weight of the internal. In many cases, there is no deep or important conflict between, for example, external non-reinforcement (no job promotions, no pay raises) and strong internal reinforcement (high self-esteem, sense of achievement, self-congratulatory celebrations). The two are complementary, and together reflect the results basis of external reinforcement and the performance basis of internal reinforcement.

Reinforcement and Motivation

Many common uses of the term "motivation" reflect a confusion between motivation and reinforcement. The two terms are indeed related; however, "motivations" are general, and "reinforcements" are specific perceived consequences. Economic necessity is a motivation for people to work, but the groceries and houses they buy are the reinforcements. Motivations, then, are the broad subjective origins of behavior; logically, they *precede* actions, causing each person to act in certain ways. Reinforcements are specific objective consequences that *follow* actions and strengthen or weaken the behavior.

Figure 3.5
Motivation, Behavior, and Reinforcement

Behavior is an objective manifestation of motivation, the appearance that motivation takes in the world. Motivations produce actions. But because motivations are internal and purely private, it is not possible, with any certainty, to work back from behavior to motive. We *infer* motivations from behavior, but we cannot observe them. Consequently, it is important to note, reinforcement is a direct response to *behavior*, but only indirectly a response to motivation. Over the long term, however, motivation can be strengthened or weakened by the consequences of an action, according to whether those consequences are positive or negative. When a behavior is positively reinforced, the original motivation is confirmed and supported—encouraging a repetition of the behavior, in the confident expectation that the reinforcement will be repeated.

You Can't Motivate Another Person

Providing external reinforcements (a typical activity of managers, teachers, and parents) has a lot to do with motivation—but it is not motivation. Strictly speaking, you *can't* motivate another person: that is, you cannot provide another person with a motivation. This fact is often concealed by our loose terminology. When managers arrange for "motivational speakers" to pep up the sales force, for instance, or when teachers speak of using grades to "motivate" student performance, the complex dynamics of motivation, behavior, and reinforcement are obscured. More precisely, managers, teachers, parents, or coaches attempt to identify the motivations of an individual that are most likely to produce desired behavior, and to offer appropriate reinforcements for the expected behavior.

Motivation and External Reinforcement

You can't motivate other people; you can, however, reinforce their behavior in the hope of confirming their own motivations. Trying to motivate people often degenerates into coaxing or cajoling—an attempt, unsupported by reinforcements, to make people behave in certain ways. The more indirect attempt to identify and support other's motivations by appropriate reinforcement is bound to be more effective—when it succeeds. For the essentially subjective nature of motivations can make it difficult to hit upon the appropriate objective reinforcements. Behavior is not always a reliable or "transparent" sign of motivation. Each individual chooses to pursue (or avoid) the reinforcements offered.

The only way to encourage a specific behavior is to create circumstances in which people will *choose* the behavior. Successful external reinforcement depends, then, on a good understanding of people's motives and preferences and an accurate estimate of the circumstances most likely to encourage a behavior. In the business world, for instance, an employer may assume that economic necessity is one of an employee's principal motivations. But there are some exceptions—and those who work for other than purely economic awards will not be affected by pay-based incentive schemes. A social worker or a minister, for example, may be primarily motivated by a desire to help others. Performance evaluations conducted in terms of monthly caseloads and savings to the welfare or health care systems, even if they are very positive, may not affect the social worker's motivation at all. Such people are not necessarily "hard to motivate"; rather, they are not being reinforced appropriately, since their motivations have not been assessed correctly. In the long run, the lack of appropriate reinforcements may weaken the desired behavior and, indirectly, diminish their original motivation.

The Contest Model

External reinforcement, then, depends on identifying motivations and devising appropriate reinforcements. Typically, the process follows what we'll call here the "contest" model. In this model, a specific behavior is encouraged by assuming a certain motivation and promising a related reward. So, for example, a sales manager might attempt to encourage increased sales activity by offering a Caribbean cruise to the sales representatives who achieve a certain level of sales. An immediate disadvantage, of course, is that not all sales reps like cruises; for them, the "motivational" scheme is a non-starter. The reinforcement will not really support behavior, and may even weaken other good motivations that, by default, are not addressed by the incentive program.

These well-intentioned schemes can easily misfire. One company president, for example, decided to reward employees who came up with money-saving and productivity ideas with a special "lunch with the president"—and was puzzled at the sudden shortage of suggestions. After a few months, he began to realize that his employees were afraid to have lunch with him: they knew him well enough to know that they didn't want to know him better. A "bonus" meant to encourage creativity and initiative had in fact operated as a disincentive; people had begun to keep their ideas to themselves.

Even the best-case possibility, in which the reinforcement is appropriate to an individual's motivation, has its drawbacks. The reinforcement drives the behavior, and it may indeed support the motivation. But when the reinforcement is gone (the year is ended and the cruise is over), there is no longer any support for either the behavior or the motivation. External reinforcements always expire—and so too does their effect on motivation. In more problematic cases (and perhaps more commonly), the reinforcement drives behavior, but has *no* effect on motivation. The contest model very easily creates a dependency on external reinforcements—and places a considerable burden on the managers or employers who use "contests" to encourage desired behavior.

The most effective use of external reinforcement occurs when a parent, teacher, or manager is able to identify, rather than assume, an individual's motivations, and to offer appropriate objective reinforcements. Directing people in this way requires talent and ability—and the process is always vulnerable to error. People's motivations are just as private and subjective as their intentions, and it is always possible to offer reinforcements that will not support a desired behavior or presumed motivation. External reinforcement may create dependency, and an endless expectation of (and demand for) more reinforcement.

Internal Reinforcement and Self-Management

The key for the self-manager is to discover one's own motivations, and to assume for oneself the role of and responsibility for self-reinforcement. Self-management depends upon recognizing and accepting these responsibilities. By internalizing *reinforcement*, self-managers replace external, transitory rewards with internal, readily available reinforcements. The motivation-behavior-reinforcement sequence becomes a self-sustaining cycle.

Figure 3.6
Ideal Relationship between Motivation, Behavior, and Reinforcement

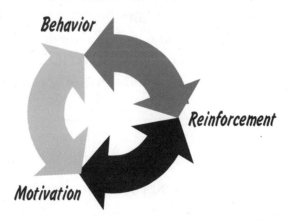

In this cycle, one's own motivation drives the behavior one decides is required; the completion of the behavior, in turn, provides the reinforcement—a feeling of satisfaction and achievement—that confirms and strengthens the original motivation. Unlike external reinforcement, which operates intermittently, constantly introducing new promises or threats to renew the approved behavior, the cycle of internal self-reinforcement operates continuously—and it is not vulnerable to changes in the external circumstances.

Self-reinforcement, then, is available *before* the results are achieved, throughout the process, and even in the face of uncontrollable obstacles. To take advantage of internal reinforcement, you need to develop strategies for reinforcing the behaviors that make up good habits, which in turn will build your success. Self-managers begin by learning to enjoy the feeling of taking control, and then learn to find the satisfaction inherent in keeping self-commitments. Ultimately, they learn to *enjoy the process*. Everyone, for instance, likes heading home from the gym *after* a workout, showered, tired, and feeling virtuous. The self-manager, however, learns to enjoy the process, the strain and effort of the workout itself, the feeling of accomplishment in the performance and process, in addition to the subsequent payoffs. An aspect of accomplishment can be discovered in even the most monotonous or routine activities, as well as in the activities that we least prefer. Internal reinforcement capitalizes on this sense of accomplishment.

YOU ONLY *HAVE* TO DO IT UNTIL YOU WANT TO DO IT;

THEN YOU DON'T *HAVE* TO DO IT ANY MORE.

Self-managers enjoy many incidental benefits from self-motivating and self-reinforcing. The supply of external reinforcements will continue—and, since self-managers are typically high achievers, those rewards may be substantial. But they are just the icing on the cake. The things people give you, believing that they are "motivating" you, are enjoyable extras to the self-manager, but they are only accidentally related to the deeper internal processes of self-reinforcement and self-determination—and the deeper, more reliable satisfaction of self-management.

90% PULL AND 10% PUSH:

THE IDEAL MOTIVATIONAL MIX

PRINCIPLE FOUR
MOTIVATE YOURSELF—OTHERS CAN'T

The Nature of Motivation

Self-management is about taking control, primarily by taking responsibility for your own performance. Self-motivation, a critical aspect of self-management, is the focus of our fourth principle. What is it, how does it operate, and why is it important to you?

There are two essential distinctions to be made concerning motivation. First, two basic modes of motivation—"push" vs "pull," or "avoidance" vs "approach"—must be separated. These oppositions seem fairly obvious, but they are not always clearly recognized, or expressed, when we consider our own actions and conduct. A second important distinction, already introduced in preceding chapters, must be made between external and internal motivation. So long as "motivation" is narrowly understood to consist in external rewards and punishments, and to be dependent upon the evaluations and behavior of others, genuine self-management will not be possible.

Modes of Motivation

Any number of factors may move a person to action. People often take action, or change their behavior, to avoid loss or pain. People will also move mountains to gain a reward or benefit or to achieve a goal.

Motivation is typically grounded in either—or both—of two impulses: fear (of failure, of unpleasant consequences) and desire (for "success," for pleasant consequences). A motive, then, may be either a "push" or a "pull," an avoidance of something or an attraction towards something. It is worth stressing this distinction, since it is not commonly observed when we consider motivation—both our own and that of others. For instance, a remark such as "I really want to get this job done!" is unmistakably an expression of commitment and determination. The remark reflects the speaker's motivation—but it doesn't tell us anything about the attitudes and effort associated with the job. There is a crucial difference between the efforts made by a person who wants to complete a job to enjoy consequential benefits, or the satisfaction of achievement, and the efforts made by a person who simply wants to have done with a job, so as to get it over with.

Figure 4.1
Ideal Motivational Mix

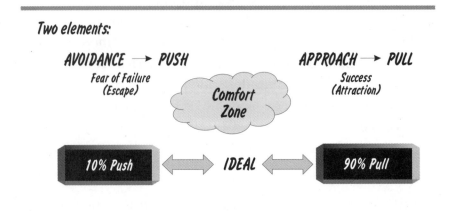

The sources of avoidance and attraction, of "push" and "pull," lie deep in personal traits and individual psychology. Every individual has a different motivational makeup. Still, some generalizations can be made. For instance, very few people are motivated purely by fear of failure. Similarly, few are impelled solely by desire for success; such extremes are atypical. Most effective self-managers have a healthy balance of avoidances and attractions. Imbalances, however, are common, and can easily be discerned in a great deal of commonplace anxiety and ennui. The underperforming student, or the employee who feels bound to the treadmill, is typically motivated by a fear of failure, and does little more than is required to escape the "punishments" that a teacher or employer can impose.

Fear of failure can be a very powerful motivation—but it can also immobilize a person, and even act as a de-motivation. Motivational makeups also vary because we all have different notions or definitions of "success" and "failure." What may seem to one person an intolerable shortcoming might strike another person as just one of the things we have to put up with in an imperfect world. A desire for achievement may also be a powerful motivation. Ambitious for success, people are capable of working very hard to make it happen.

"Push" and "Pull" Motivation

Managers, teachers, and parents would often like to know what balance of "push" and "pull" motivation is "best," or more effective. Should there be more fear of failure, or more desire for success? There is no simple answer. Every person works out his or her own balance between "push" and "pull"—an individual "comfort zone." After all, motivation lies within; that is why a person cannot really be "motivated" by others, but only reinforced. The difference between "push" and "pull," however, is easily observed. Consider two possible views of mortgage payments. A "push"-oriented person is likely to say, "If I miss this payment I could lose my house"; a "pull"-oriented person will say, "This month's payment brings me that much closer to owning the house." Or consider two approaches to health: are you afraid of getting sick, or do you want to feel strong and fit? Both motivations could lead to the same specific behavior or action—but the attitudes and approaches that go along with the two perspectives will differ significantly.

Obviously, the "pull"-oriented person's attitudes are more positive. This doesn't necessarily mean that "pull" is more effective than "push"—but it is certainly less stressful. This was illustrated for us at a conference for top-performing insurance company salespeople. We asked the agents whether they believed themselves to be externally or internally motivated; the vast majority considered themselves to be internally motivated. Then we asked whether they were motivated mainly by "push" or by "pull": only one-third opted for "push," and the remaining two-thirds claimed to be "pull-motivated." All of the agents were high achievers, but they differed with regard to the nature of their motivation. One self-confessed "push-motivated" agent put it like this: "I have just completed a very successful year, but all I think of is, how can I ever do it again? Where will the business come from? I feel a lot of pressure, even though I've done pretty well!" By contrast, a "pull-motivated" agent said, "I'm excited about the past year, and I'm looking forward to doing even more next year." This suggests the benefits of "pull" over "push." In fact, we would suggest that the ideal motivational mix is about 90% "pull" and 10% "push."

The attitudinal benefits of "pull" motivation can be seen most clearly in "motivational breakthroughs"—points at which a person shifts from avoidance to approach.

These breakthroughs are easily illustrated. Consider, for example, the breakthrough point on the long drive to the cottage, when the avoidance feelings of getting away from the city and the traffic are replaced by the positive anticipation of arriving at your destination. Suddenly, everything changes: attitudes and perceptions all shift from avoidance to attraction. Suddenly, you are approaching the cottage, not leaving the city.

Figure 4.2
Approach/Avoidance Conflict

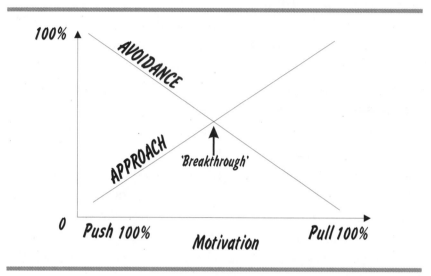

Motivational breakthroughs, in which "push" gives way to "pull," represent the moments when motivation is at its highest: they refresh and renew effort and commitment. And it is possible to tap their power. These moments do not just occur; they can be engineered. The halfway point of a long drive is a fairly "natural" breakpoint, but there is no reason that you could not *set* breakpoints earlier—"Now I'm out of the city limits"; "No more commuter traffic: I'm north of Highway 89"; and so on.

Of course, we use strategies like this all the time—it's part of coping. Unfortunately, we are inclined to underestimate their importance. In the back of our minds, a nagging doubt remains:

aren't we just kidding ourselves? So we're halfway to the halfway point: we aren't *there* yet. This scepticism proceeds directly from our customary fixation on *results*. Yes: what really counts is covering the distance. But we will never make it unless we can find ways to make it bearable, worthwhile, even satisfying. The *process* we set up for ourselves is enormously valuable as a means of *performance*.

Self-managers recognize the power of these strategies. They enjoy motivational breakthroughs by focusing on the stages of progress and performance, as well as on completion and the final result. They create a continued series of moments at which "push" and "pull" approach the optimal 10/90 ratio. Self-managers are well-motivated, not because they have the "best" motivations, but because they know their motivations best. That is, they develop and maintain an awareness of how they respond in terms of "push" and "pull" motivations. More importantly, they use that self-knowledge to take responsibility for their own motivation. They take charge of the "will-do" component of performance—a crucial component, as the performance equation illustrates.

External and Internal Motivation

The combination of "push" and "pull" motivations that you prefer (or perhaps need) may not always be offered by the actual circumstances of your family life, school, society, or work. Mismatches between an individual's motivational makeup and the external circumstances can have painful effects—when only external motivations, or, to be more precise, external *reinforcements*—punishments or rewards—are operative. When every reason to act comes from outside, either as a kind of threat or a kind of bribe, it is easy to become dissatisfied with success, and even perversely pleased by failure ("They loused it up again"; after all, if all motivation is external, nothing is *your* responsibility).

Whether "push" or "pull," external motivations necessarily have short-term effects. External motivations typically lose their power as we move away from the negative possibilities that "frightened" us into action, or move towards the positive expectations that attracted us. In the case of a "push" motivation, the farther you get from the threatening negatives, the less motivated you become. "Pull" motivation similarly declines—as you approach the payoff. The student who works hard only to avoid failing will usually be satisfied with a "D," since at that point the force of the threat evaporates. Similarly, the attractive force of promised rewards is exhausted once they are attained. Last month's performance benefit has little effect on *this* month's efforts, for instance. Similarly, wanting to lose ten pounds can keep you dieting and exercising, but once the weight is lost, the original motivation—wanting to lose ten pounds—disappears.

"PUSH" MOTIVATIONS KEEP YOU LOOKING BACK,

WHERE YOU HAVE BEEN.

"PULL" MOTIVATIONS KEEP YOU WORKING FORWARD,

TO WHERE YOU ARE GOING.

Business provides many examples of the inefficiency of external motivations. Consider the salesperson who, on the verge of failing, is put on probation: he has 60 days to meet a quota, or he will lose his job. This sort of practice is common enough. However, if the salesperson hits the externally imposed quota, he reaches a temporary "comfort zone." The threat of unemployment is left behind, and any other encouragements or inducements to exceed the quota fall on deaf ears. The immediate threat has passed.

People who are primarily motivated by externals, and who don't provide their own reasons for continued effort and growth, are likely to ride a roller coaster of highs and lows. Results are inconsistent and, in the vernacular of the sales world, it's "feast or famine." Anyone in sales will tell you that making your way up the hills and down the valleys is extremely stressful. No one can do it for long; burn-out soon follows.

External motivations, then, provide little in the way of lasting satisfactions. They require constant external management to be successful—and they also require a constant escalation of rewards. As soon as they are achieved, they no longer possess any genuine attraction—and the suspicion is that something else, something better, has been withheld. External motivation can only succeed by constantly "upping the ante," promising more and better rewards to those "who stay the course." (This is a common feature of corporate employment, but it is also well-known to any parent who has paid a child a dollar to run an errand; the price is sure to double for the next job.) Almost every external motivation, too, is ultimately reducible to purely material terms, a quantity of "consumer non-durables" that, once consumed, leaves no traces.

We are conditioned to accept and even to welcome external motivation. The mechanisms of external control are established early on. Children learn to perform in accepted or desired ways in response to positive and negative reinforcements. External commands are followed by external consequences. Students learn by rote in roughly the same way, and later are motivated by praise and blame to undertake more challenging assignments. The process continues in a wide variety of adult contexts: as employees, voters, and consumers, we are urged by influential authorities to act in certain ways so as to avoid undesirable situations or to enjoy attractive benefits. The mechanisms of external control continue to operate throughout our lives. As noted, every single external attempt at motivation is short-lived, and once it is exhausted, it must be followed by another. But the conventional structures of family, society, work, and politics satisfy the requirement for endlessly renewed external motives. It is seldom literally true that a person "does not know what to do"—there is no shortage of people and institutions ready to provide that information. It is true, fortunately, that people can resist the many and often conflicting sources of external authority long enough to open a question of "what to do."

"Internal Never Stops": The Power of Internal Motivation

The more one responds to external motivations, or other people's reasons to do something, the more one runs the risk of losing sight of the real reason for doing or accomplishing something—internal reinforcement, achievement, and deep personal satisfaction. The power of internal motivation is easily observed: just look at your own successes. In our society, learning to write is common enough—although it is an enormously complex and difficult cognitive accomplishment. The success most of us have in acquiring a host of language concepts and manual skills necessarily depends on internal motivation. We begin to learn to write by rote, tracing letterforms and imitating sound patterns, in response to external motivations. But writing really begins when the activity works from the inside out—when we write to express an internal intention.

The power of internal motivation can also be seen in those whom we consider successful. Top-performing athletes, for instance, obviously enjoy huge financial rewards, but they all agree that their prime motivation is a sense of accomplishment, a constant pursuit of individual excellence. The greatest business successes also depend more on internal motivation and reinforcement than on external rewards.

Breaking Loose

Self-managers have broken loose from the endlessly renewed cycle of external motivation. They replace the typically material inducements provided from outside, rapidly exhausted and incessantly renewed, with internal motivations that are never-ending and constantly reinforcing. For many people, "being managed" is the norm. Self-managers recognize the limitations of this view. They know that "being managed" is an inevitable part of our lives, but they find ways to motivate themselves, from within. They seek the feeling of success and the accompanying sense of competence—a success that depends not on other people's constantly shifting criteria, but on their own goals and purposes, developed with self-knowledge and self-determination. Internal motivations, whether they involve a "push" or a "pull," can offer genuine satisfaction. Achieving the goals one proposes for oneself is very different from competing for the prizes others set out.

THE ONLY LONG-TERM MOTIVATOR
OF HUMAN BEHAVIOR IS A
SENSE OF COMPETENCE.

That "success breeds success" is well understood by the self-manager. The feelings of success and competence are—and this bears repeating—never-ending and constantly reinforcing. People like to do, and will do, what they feel they do well, and they will tackle bigger challenges and opportunities where an expectation of success or a feeling of capability exists. In fact, we will continually repeat what we think we do well until we forget that we do it well.

ROE: THREE STEPS

1) ESTABLISH COMMITMENT AREAS.

2) SET PRIORITIES.

3) MANAGE ENERGY WITHIN COMMITMENT AREAS.

PRINCIPLE FIVE
MAXIMIZE RETURN ON ENERGY (ROE)

The Secret of Happiness

Self-managers are, typically, robust people: they are energetic, successful, satisfied, and productive. There are many reasons for this characteristic vigor. But essentially, those happy, healthy people are people who get good returns on the energy and effort they expend. Most of us have our own ideas about where effort is best directed, and there are any number of ways in which we can realize a good return on our energy. In this sense, satisfaction has to do with how you perceive your efforts and achievements, and what sort of return you feel you are getting on the effort you put out.

Burn-Out = Poor Return on Energy

People's *perceptions* of their efforts and achievements are also central to the phenomenon of "burn-out." Burn-out can be quickly defined as a poor *perceived* return on an investment of energy. Think, for example, of a time in your career when it seemed that fate was against you—that every road led to a roadblock. Your hard work was going unnoticed, and the results you anticipated did not materialize. The resulting frustration and discouragement could have led to reduced confidence and diminished expectations; you might even have felt like giving up trying. You were beginning the process of burn-out.

Burn-out is often observed in the working world, where it has come to be recognized as an occupational hazard—in pretty well *any* occupation. Low effort levels, reduced enthusiasm, and diminished job satisfaction are the classical symptoms of burn-out. And it cuts across every hierarchy; everyone is vulnerable. Burn-out is often considered to be primarily a business and management problem, but it occurs in any of the activities that make up our lives, and in any context where people keep commitments, make efforts, and pursue objectives: relationships, family life, volunteer work, school, exercise, sport. When the results of a person's actions don't appear to measure up to his or her effort, attitudes and happiness are diminished. As the process of burn-out takes its course (and it may do so very quickly), the victim becomes increasingly unwilling to renew his or her efforts. Perhaps more importantly, the sufferer becomes increasingly likely to undervalue his or her returns, which accelerates the downward spiral.

Calculating Returns on Energy (ROE): Lifestyle Analysis

A sense of self-worth and happiness, then, depends not only on what you do, but on how you assess it. Correctly evaluating your investments and returns is crucial—and often challenging! First, it is not a simple calculation: a variety of factors must be considered. Second, it is easy to under- or overestimate the quantity and quality of the energy you commit to activities. And finally, it is not always easy to identify your returns accurately.

Lifestyle analysis helps clarify the terms in which accurate ROE calculations can be made. Analysis begins by distinguishing "commitment areas" and the amount of energy devoted to each one. In a simple analysis, as few as three or four areas may suffice. More complex analyses may also take into account a wider range of specific kinds of commitment—community, church, recreation, and so on.

Figure 5.1
Commitment Areas and Percentage of Energy

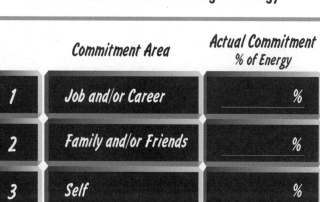

	Commitment Area	Actual Commitment % of Energy
1	Job and/or Career	_____ %
2	Family and/or Friends	_____ %
3	Self	_____ %
	Total	100%

Time vs Energy

It is usually quite easy to identify your commitment areas. However, lifestyle analysis is often sidetracked by a common confusion between *time* and *energy*. That is, people often identify what they spend the most time at, and establish their priorities accordingly (see Figure 5.2).

Deriving priorities from the amount of time a person spends on various activities encourages a process of *time-managing* priorities, as opposed to *self-managing* energy. If we believe that our priorities are indeed revealed by our timetables, the quite common allocation of time shown in Figure 5.2 is not only misleading: it creates self-doubt and guilt. The time analysis reflects the simple fact in our society that most of us spend most of our time on our work. And work certainly has a high priority for us. But the sample in Figure 5.2 also forces us to

Figure 5.2
Commitment Areas and Time Management

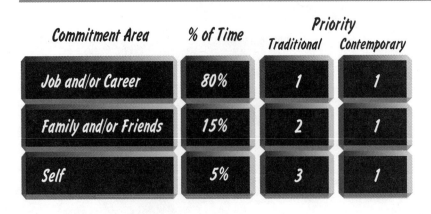

Commitment Area	% of Time	Priority Traditional	Contemporary
Job and/or Career	80%	1	1
Family and/or Friends	15%	2	1
Self	5%	3	1

believe that our families, and even ourselves, are *lower* in priority. That doesn't seem right!—but that's what the figures show. As a result, we are likely to feel guilty, and to try to compensate those we have apparently been neglecting. Typically, such attempts create even more stress: the busy entrepreneur who takes a day off to "catch up" with her family will find even more work backed up when she returns, and will have to spend even more time catching up—and so will spend less time with family, and so on. This sort of dilemma is caused by choosing the wrong terms for lifestyle analysis. Actual adjustments—and improvements—can be made when we deal, not with time management and priorities, but with self-management and energy.

Effective Lifestyle Management

Lifestyle management requires that we distinguish between the amount of energy that is invested and the amount of time that is spent in an activity. This confusion is especially common in business, where a quantitative, results-oriented approach is the norm. In business, it is very easy to allow one's calculations of returns on energy to be replaced by calculations of returns on time spent: "working hard" is replaced by "working long." Everyone knows it is possible to make a significant effort in a short time—but long work hours, overtime, weekend work, "face" time, and the like can be recorded, documented objectively, while an individual's actual effort levels remain internal and largely unobservable.

However, it's not just in business that people appraise their efforts by calculating their returns—and in any context, it is possible to mistake how much time we spend for how much energy we invest. After all, "I have to spend more time on/with/at..." is how we commonly express our intention to make a greater effort in an activity, a relationship, or a commitment. But, because such calculations are skewed by factoring in time rather than energy, a perception of poor returns is very likely.

Effective lifestyle management depends on a self-management process:

---

1) ESTABLISH COMMITMENT AREAS.

2) SET PRIORITIES.

3) MANAGE ENERGY WITHIN COMMITMENT AREAS.

Lifestyle analysis shows where investments can best be made, and where it is possible to increase returns. Such analysis must be based on an accurate estimate of the physical and mental energy that goes into each area, as opposed to the time that is spent in various activities. Calculating the returns on time, rather than energy, usually obscures the true value of the investment, since you are applying an external measure to an internal activity. It's tempting to do so, because measuring time (an external) provides very precise values for our calculations—it seems a more reliable, objective approach. But this objectivity is misplaced. The amount of energy we invest in any enterprise or activity can only be known, with certainty, to ourselves—and we cannot express it in terms of time. Estimating effort (an internal) provides less precise, but more accurate, input for the lifestyle model.

An analysis in terms of *energy* still needs to be interpreted correctly. Consider the following example:

Figure 5.3
Commitment Areas and Satisfaction

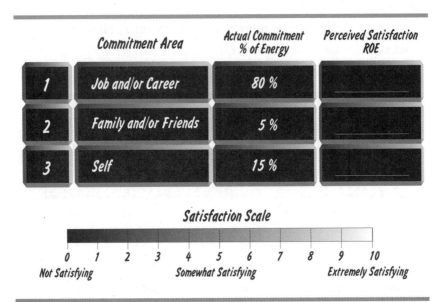

	Commitment Area	Actual Commitment % of Energy	Perceived Satisfaction ROE
1	Job and/or Career	80 %	
2	Family and/or Friends	5 %	
3	Self	15 %	

Satisfaction Scale

0 1 2 3 4 5 6 7 8 9 10

Not Satisfying   Somewhat Satisfying   Extremely Satisfying

Even before the returns are entered, such an analysis might provoke some dismay or misgiving: look at how little the family got (much less than you gave yourself)! Why was so huge a proportion devoted to work?

This sort of self-questioning follows from *misreading* the chart. Assessments of your energy allocations will vary from day to day. Some days, you may devote no energy to a commitment area. The reason it *seems* wrong is that we tend to see these allocations as an index of our priorities. So, if you find yourself giving more energy to yourself than to your family, you may feel that you are giving yourself a higher priority.

This response ignores a crucial fact: you only have so much energy. If 80 per cent gets used at work, there is only 20 per cent left for other commitments. The important thing, then, is to use the energy you have left, making sure that no important commitment area is left unaddressed—and feel good about what you do achieve, rather than feel guilty about what you really *couldn't* achieve that day.

Assessing Returns

The energy allocations you use in your lifestyle analysis, then, do not "reveal" your priorities. Your priorities are determined *first*, as in Figure 5.4. According to the priorities you set, you attempt to manage your energy. The lifestyle analysis, then, shows you *how well* you are managing, and lets you determine where and how to adjust your efforts to improve your quality of life. It does so by showing *returns* on energy invested.

Often, because we are conditioned to expect (and require) external motivation, we add up only the "returns" that consist of external reinforcements. As a result, we may consider that our returns—that is, the rewards conferred by others, the objective results—are not proportionate to our effort. Nor are they easily compared; there is no "exchange rate" that makes it possible to find a meaningful relation between efforts and various sorts of return.

Figure 5.4
Commitment Areas and Lifestyle Management

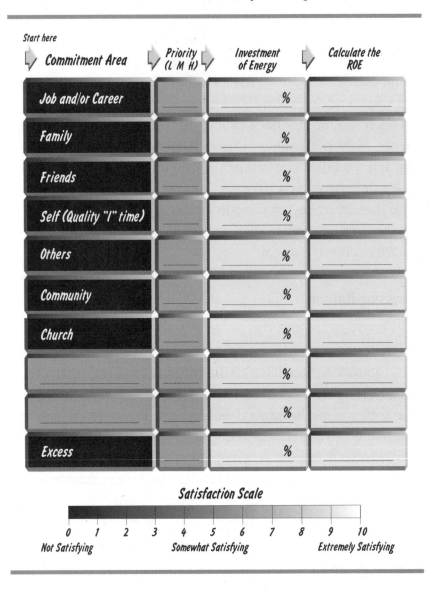

Figure 5.5
Commitment Areas and External Influences

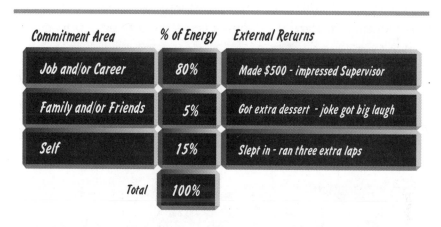

Commitment Area	% of Energy	External Returns
Job and/or Career	80%	Made $500 - impressed Supervisor
Family and/or Friends	5%	Got extra dessert - joke got big laugh
Self	15%	Slept in - ran three extra laps
Total	100%	

Figure 5.5 shows a correlation between high effort and high returns at work—the sort of correlation we tend to take for granted. But we all know that on some days, hard work goes unnoticed by the rest of the world, and that external returns may be very low. And it is just as common for rewards to exceed effort: in Figure 5.5, a low investment of energy in family and friends has a considerable return.

A robust self-manager combines the external and internal reinforcements. Only you really know how much of an effort you make—and only you know how it makes you feel to make the effort. Internal feelings of success, achievement, satisfaction, accomplishment, and completion all represent a valuable return on effort expended. The student who tries hard but gets a "C" on the final exam can't expect his effort to be part of the teacher's final grade—but it should certainly count in his own self-appraisal. Similarly, a salesperson who misses the weekly sales goal—and hears about it from the sales manager—may be able to balance the disappointing results against several successful first meetings, a promising presentation to a potentially large account, and a good number of new contacts. When you add *efforts* to the assessment, you can often know and feel that you are winning—even thought the world hasn't noticed yet.

Figure 5.6
Calculating Returns on Energy (ROE)

External Factors	Internal Factors
Rewards	Satisfaction
Punishments	Positive Self-evaluation
Payoffs	Sense of Accomplishment
Congratulations	Sense of Success
Praise	Sense of Completion

The challenge for the self-manager, then, is to recognize the "returns" that are available in the process, as well as the returns others provide for the results. Finding the returns *within the process* allows a self-manager to maintain the effort needed to attain the objective, real-world results.

Including the internal reinforcements creates an accurate estimate of the returns. It also allows a balance of external responses to complement our sense of our strengths and resources. Highly talented people, for instance, are likely to receive approval even when they make less than their full effort. If they are not strong self-managers, this external reinforcement may be accepted at face value, perhaps causing them to maintain less-than-optimum effort levels: they allow externals to outweigh internals. In the long term, their chances of success are reduced. Good self-managers "find the returns." That is, they identify and emphasize the internal, as well as the external, consequences of their actions. They tend to be healthier and happier, not because all the good things happen to them, but because they invest their effort wisely, and have a better appreciation of their returns.

Quality of Life

A properly developed, properly interpreted lifestyle analysis shows what is working well and what can be improved in our energy management (see Figure 5.7). Returns, properly understood as both internal and external, are difficult to quantify precisely; relative proportions are a more convenient means to express returns and compare them to energy investments. The sample analysis in Figure 5.7 shows how ROE calculations can be made. The chart reflects a situation, but also suggests ways to improve the quality of life. One is to put more energy into high-return areas; you can be sure that the extra input will be rewarded. The other is to improve returns in areas that are capable of growth, usually by changing activities and procedures, or working on communication and relationships. The analysis also indicates where energy should be conserved: trying to improve a lifestyle by putting energy into obviously low-return areas will only take energy away from areas with better potential.

Figure 5.7
Commitment Areas and Quality of Life

Self-Assessment

Commitment Area	Actual Commitment % of Energy		Perceived Satisfaction ROE		Total
Job and/or Career	70%	X	5	=	350
Family and/or Friends	20%	X	8	=	160
Self	10%	X	6	=	60
				Total	570

Satisfaction Scale

0   1   2   3   4   5   6   7   8   9   10

Not Satisfying   Somewhat Satisfying   Extremely Satisfying

Lifestyle Possibilities: R > E, R = E, R < E

Lifestyle analysis can help identify areas in which investments of energy are not balanced or exceeded by returns—areas in which your health and happiness are most vulnerable. There are three basic possibilities.

1. **Returns > effort: You are "on a roll"—returns perceptibly exceed your investments of energy.**

2. **Returns = effort: You are holding on, maintaining a level balance— that's good, but the balance you have achieved is fragile.**

3. **Returns < effort: You are putting in more than you are getting back: you may very well be on the way to burn-out.**

ROE calculations provide one of the quickest and surest ways to assess our achievements from day to day, and even moment to moment. And the results of such calculations have a pronounced effect on our attitudes, motivations, and commitments.

R > E: "On a Roll"

When returns seem to exceed energy expended, our investments seem to be paying off. Satisfaction levels are high, and attitudes are strengthened—a combination that sustains good efforts and compounds the gains. Realizing a good return is often the beginning of a "winning streak," since a feeling of success and productivity will tend to sustain itself. The difference between energy and returns needn't be a large one: just a little "extra" is enough to reassure us that progress and growth can be continuous. A jogger who finds she can add an extra lap to her daily run, for example, may not be ready for the marathon—but she will feel that she is on the way, and will keep making an effort. Coaches know this too. The greatest gains in conditioning and skills are typically made during a winning streak, and when things are going well, teams and players practice their hardest, with high expectations of success.

Good returns affect every element of performance. One of the most important effects is to improve attitudes and effort, but a good return also influences our perceptions of our abilities and strengths. High self-esteem makes us positive and robust. When we feel that returns exceed energy, we have increased confidence in the abilities we know we possess—and we are also encouraged to develop new competencies. Together, strengthened attitudes and abilities support development and growth. If you feel that you have a good foundation of strengths and a positive attitude, it is much easier to consider where you should invest energy in skills development, or where you might increase performance by changing some aspect of opportunity. Good returns also change the way we perceive our opportunity and environment. A good return on energy when we work, play, or study feeds back into the environment we create, strengthening it, and increasing the chance of further worthwhile investments of effort.

ENTHUSIASM IS CONTAGIOUS, AND SO IS THE LACK OF IT.

The renewed energy that one person brings to his or her efforts can invigorate everyone in a group, but only one or two naysayers can, in some cases, slow them down again. This synergism can be observed in many areas. In sports, for instance, energy levels are boosted by every score in an exciting, hard-fought game; everyone is caught up in a self-reinforcing effort. Competition keeps players sharp, especially when they are playing up to a stronger competitor.

E = R: Holding On

When energy and effort appear to balanced by returns, people are generally quite fragile: they depend on recent, local events for their feelings. A certain amount of satisfaction is available when you feel that you are getting as much out of an activity or an enterprise as you are putting in. But the long-term effects of this sort of balance are vulnerable. First, there are limits to the satisfaction it offers. After all, we make investments in the hope of gains. More importantly, a strict equality of investment and return does not strengthen the attitudes that underlie effort. Instead, attitudes become fragile and easily unsettled. When returns just balance energy, little things easily affect moods and attitudes. Things proceed on a day-to-day basis, and every momentary fluctuation receives more than its due share of attention.

R < E: Burn-Out

When we perceive that our energy and effort exceed returns, we are likely to feel that we have made a bad investment, and to question the value of our efforts. Unless we change the situation, the process of burn-out begins. When we work hard, but the desired results just don't seem to occur, attitudes are affected. We may become discouraged or frustrated; eventually, we may even give up trying. Our sense of our abilities and strengths may also suffer. When internal and external responses do not provide the requisite satisfaction, it is very easy to doubt our skills. Failing to perform a task or meet a challenge, for example, often leads us to make all-or-nothing judgments: "I keep getting rejected—nobody will give me an appointment. I guess selling just isn't for me." Categorical judgments like these undermine confidence and tend to make us consciously incompetent. Our perceptions of opportunity and environment are also affected: it may seem that effort is pointless, since the circumstances are all against us.

Burn-out doesn't happen all at once. As a process, it begins with the perception of a poor return of effort, which leads us to question our efforts, our environment, and our talents. If there is no improvement, attitudes worsen. Effort may be sustained for some time; we might continue to work hard. But without good returns, we will eventually stop, taking the fatalistic position that effort is pointless: it's all determined elsewhere, by others and by circumstances.

WE STOP DOING THINGS THAT ARE

NEGATIVELY REINFORCED.

Self-Management and ROE Calculations

Some people always seem to be robust and energetic. It's as though they always get a good return on their investments, and are somehow invulnerable to burn-out. They are usually very successful in worldly terms, it's worth noting—popular, well-employed, well-paid. But their happiness consists in more than just the external reinforcements—economic rewards, employer's approval, colleagues' admiration. They are self-managers: they have a balanced lifestyle, and, because they manage their energy within their commitment areas, they have a high quality of life. They maximize ROE, focusing on the positives, and include both internal and external reinforcements in their ongoing ROE calculations. It's difficult to say whether they are happy because they are successful or successful because they are happy. Self-managers are careful to measure their efforts (which they are in a unique position to judge) against their own sense of achievement or completion.

Internal, performance-based ROE evaluations, combined with the results-based calculations made by oneself and others, provide self-managing individuals with assessments that are more complete and more reliable as a foundation for continued effort. Self-managers can evaluate their progress, even when others have not yet seen the results. On the basis of their achievements, self-managers work towards the results that finally bring them external rewards and positive reinforcement from without. But, as mentioned in Chapter Three, these external reinforcements are additional benefits, add-ons—nice to have, but not essential to the self-manager.

Happiness on Your Own Terms

For each performance element, the effort, ability, or opportunity factored into ROE calculations is never fixed, but is based upon the perceptions of the individual. Many people are tired and fragile because their perceived returns are less than or equal to their investment of energy. Excitement and energy, however, lie within. Those who are happy and fulfilled have learned where to seek their genuine satisfactions—not only in others' appraisals, which cannot adequately recognize an individual's performance, but also internally, in the fitting proportion of their initiatives and their accomplishments.

THERE IS ONLY ONE WAY

TO GET FROM OBJECTIVES TO RESULTS—

EFFORT.

PRINCIPLE SIX
MANAGE EFFORT

Getting Results

We have stressed that self-managers take responsibility for their *performance* and remain *accountable* for their results. There's no way around it: results pay the bills.

We use results to assess people's character and accomplishments, both our own and others'. It is essential for us, then, to set up specific objectives as the goals towards which we work. A "goal" or "objective" is characteristically expressed in terms of the results we wish to achieve. Setting goals and measuring our results according to those goals is one of the key ways in which we motivate ourselves and make decisions about what we could achieve in the future.

THERE IS ONLY ONE WAY

TO GET FROM OBJECTIVES TO RESULTS—

EFFORT.

Study after study—as well as common sense—shows that successful people work hard or have worked hard. The common characteristic of most successful people is effort! We work *towards* results and objectives, but at any given moment in the process, we must manage effort—it's the one thing that we can manage.

Controllables and Non-controllables

It is critically important to set objectives and evaluate results. However, attempting to manage oneself by results or objectives alone often leads to crisis management, if the desired goals are not attained. Objectives and results offer specific, well-defined reference points, but managing by objectives and results easily becomes a matter of reacting to circumstances rather than progressing towards goals. When you are working to reach established objectives, you are vulnerable to any number of non-controllable factors that can delay or even prevent the desired outcome. Therefore, the only effective way to achieve objectives and results is to focus on and take control of controllables. Attempting to take control of the non-controllables will lead to stress and eventually to burn-out. Taking control of the controllables, however, gives you the best chance for success and the results you want.

The quick solution is to manage effort, and manage the controllables that will create the best possible results. Self-management begins with a recognition of the uncontrollable and controllable components of achieving results. Self-managers ensure that the focus remains on progress, first by distinguishing between controllables and non-controllables, and then by taking control of the controllables. This involves a good awareness of the external circumstances, but it is also an exercise in self-knowledge. For our perception of the controllables is not always accurate. Unless we manage by effort, it is easy to believe ourselves capable of much less—or in some cases much more—than really lies within our power.

In a workshop on the sales process that we conducted some years ago, we asked the top-performing sales rep, "Bert, can you guarantee a sale today?" Bert said "No"—and the rookies in the room reacted with disbelief and some concern. "If Bert can't guarantee a sale today, what am I doing in this business?" they seemed to be thinking. We asked Bert why not. His answer was full of insight and the wisdom of years of experience: "Somebody else decides that," he said. When asked whether he could make enough calls that day to reach ten people, he responded quickly, "Yes, absolutely."

Self-managers typically have an accurate, realistic perception of the controllables. They are notably successful, not because they can do anything they want to, but because they do what they need to do. Like everybody else, self-managers have limits—but they know where these limits really lie. Knowing what they can do, they can allocate their energy and efforts effectively, concentrating on the aspects of performance within their control.

Integrating Objectives, Effort, and Results

Self-managers understand the active process that links objectives to results. After all, there is only one way to move from objectives to results, and that is through effort. Managing by objectives and managing by results are part of this process, but they must take their proper place in a more fully developed system.

Self-managers begin by setting their own objectives—often after consultation or negotiation with a coach or manager. Setting objectives is the first phase of the process. The self-manager has a good idea of what he or she wants (or needs) to accomplish, and can put it in realistic terms. After all, as it has been said, "If you don't know where you're going, any road will take you there."

In addition to assessing the objectives and quantifying the final result, the self-manager also sets out and commits himself or herself to a series of specific, well-devised efforts. Managing

Figure 6.1
Integrating Objectives, Effort, and Results

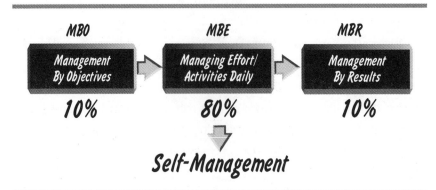

these efforts, or interim initiatives, occupies by far the largest proportion of the self-manager's time and attention. The process is defined and organized in terms of the steps in the process—since, in order to achieve the best results, effort must be directed towards the controllables. Trying to take control of non-controllables is ineffective, wastes effort, and creates stress. Because the process can be divided into distinct stages, it is possible—and necessary—to evaluate performance at each stage and to develop strategies for improvement. The *end result* is now the product of a series of *interim results:*

Figure 6.2
Results vs End Result

Managing by results is part of the process, but it is postponed until the end result has been achieved. At that point, the process may be assessed as a whole. Up to that point, however, the process is constantly assessed in terms of effectiveness and progress toward the end result. Then, of course, the end results are compared to the initial objectives. This allows a simple "pass/fail" judgment on whether or not performance achieved the desired results. At the same time, however, the self-manager has been reviewing the detailed progression of efforts that produced the results.

Assessing results—at the proper time—is an important part of the self-management process. When objectives and results match, both performance, as evaluated internally, and results, as judged by the world, are satisfactory. Positive reinforcement, both internal and external, follows more or less automatically, and strengthens the successful process.

Figure 6.3
Results vs End Result: Practical Example

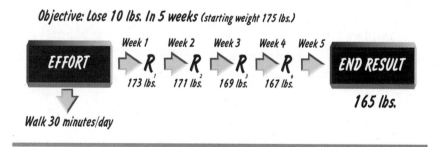

Objective: Lose 10 lbs. In 5 weeks (starting weight 175 lbs.)

	Week 1	Week 2	Week 3	Week 4	Week 5	
EFFORT	R_1	R_2	R_3	R_4		END RESULT
	173 lbs.	171 lbs.	169 lbs.	167 lbs.		165 lbs.

Walk 30 minutes/day

Figure 6.3 illustrates the way in which a *process* can link specific, feasible efforts to produce an end result. The sense of achievement that is available at each step drives the process to completion. And at every point, a sense of progress ("pull" motivation) supports the commitment.

When Objectives and Results Don't Match

Self-managers are never really surprised when objectives and results don't match; they will always have seen it coming. When the end results turn out to be better than expected, it can be seen to be more than a matter of luck. Self-managers generally anticipate the bonus, and can identify the strategies and controllable elements that contribute to it. As a result, the success can be duplicated. And if it seems that a shortfall is likely, self-managers will already have made efforts to bring their activities back on track and to reduce the effects of the mismatch. They can adjust at any point in the process, rather than "waiting to see how things turn out." As a result, an unwelcome difference between objectives and results can often be moderated, and the self-manager will approach his or her next initiative on the basis of what has been learned.

Management by Results

For people who manage exclusively by objectives, or by results, however, it is always a surprise when objectives and results do not match—usually a nasty one. Unexpected shortfalls appear as catastrophes: we look for who or what is to blame, and switch into crisis management mode. But crisis management is directed towards something that has already happened.

Figure 6.4
Management by Crisis

Results are history: they show you where you went, not where you should be going. The "dreaded why" that turns obsessively *back* in a futile search for a reason, an excuse, or an explanation is fatal to progress. After all, *results count:* if you didn't get the results you need, an analysis of your failure is hardly an acceptable substitute.

As a result, divergences between objectives and results usually have damaging long-term consequences for those who manage by either one—even when results are better than expected. The difference can be celebrated, but not duplicated. People generally recognize, more or less consciously, that results cannot be fully controlled. Objectives, however, are entirely within our control. Typically, then, objectives are revised upwards or downwards in light of the results actually achieved; this revision tends either to inflate or deflate expectations.

Even when results do satisfy objectives, those who manage by objectives or by results do not derive the full benefits of their success. A match between stated objectives and the results can be taken at face value, as a kind of validation of the objectives. Things go well, but no one really knows *why*. The tendency then is to "lock in" the expectations, and keep on doing the same things again and again—the characteristic feature of unconscious competence. If you know you can achieve a specific result by carrying out a well-established routine, you may not be very motivated to reset your goals or to reconsider your process. Old accustomed routines can be very reassuring—but they offer little potential for growth.

Managing by effort, then, allows you to moderate failures and to improve on successes. Differences between objectives and results do not come as catastrophic surprises, and do not require drastic revisions of your objectives. Instead, the self-manager can re-examine the successive steps of the process that links objectives and results, fine-tuning the individual efforts that make up the process.

WHEN YOU KNOW WHEN, WHY,

AND HOW YOU ACHIEVED A GOOD RESULT,

YOU WILL BE ABLE TO DO IT THE NEXT TIME.

AND YOU WILL PROBABLY DO IT *BETTER*.

Self-managers—and those around them—are also spared the necessity of excuses, should the results not measure up. Excuses typically refer (in more or less pathetic detail) to the *non-controllables* that delayed or prevented the desired results; they seldom touch on the nature of the performance that led to the results. Self-managers commit themselves to controlling the controllables. While they cannot make *excuses* for a failure to achieve established objectives, they can *explain* the failure in terms of talent, effort, and opportunity. And, when results exceed objectives, self-managers need not discount the success as sheer good luck. They can identify the controllable aspects that created the good results, and further develop their conscious competence. No matter what the results, then, self-managers can devise strategies for improved performance.

Improving Performance—and Results

Managing by effort offers four strategies for increasing performance.

- WORK MORE CONSISTENTLY

- WORK HARDER (QUANTITY)

- WORK SMARTER (QUALITY)

- WORK HARDER AND SMARTER
  (QUANTITY AND QUALITY)

All four strategies allow you to take control of the controllables by concentrating on the elements of performance.

1. Work More Consistently

The easiest strategy is simply to make more consistent efforts on a more consistent basis. This requires little more than a sustained commitment to a *quantity* of effort. You don't have to change what you are doing; you just have to do more of it. Nevertheless, the potential effectiveness is obvious. Anyone trying to get into shape, for instance, knows that satisfying results are bound to be improved by a regular exercise program. The crucial step is to make the required effort a habit. Given a long enough time frame, just twenty minutes a day will take care of any project, no matter how difficult or disagreeable. When the effort is made consistently, a person avoids a roller coaster of highs and lows, and develops a process that is consistent and habitual.

2. Work Harder (Quantity)

A second strategy is to work harder. Depending on current effort levels, this may be a more challenging approach, but it will have a direct impact on performance and a longer-term impact on results. It also has to do with the quantifiable aspects of effort. Your activities remain the same, but you increase the amount and the intensity. For instance, the results of a daily exercise program may be improved by increasing the duration, intensity, or number of workouts (30 minutes rather than 20, for instance, or 15-pound weights rather than 10). Working harder also yields the benefits of "compound improvement." Small gains in effort do not just add to performance, but, like compound interest, create large improvements in performance. Working harder, then, involves small, feasible adjustments that can, in the long term, bring about significant changes in performance and results.

3. Work Smarter (Quality)

A third strategy is to improve results by working smarter—changing the *quality*, rather than the quantity, of effort. Such a strategy often takes more time, and is less direct in its effects, than making adjustments to the quantity of effort. Working smarter involves making changes to the things you do and the way you do them. It involves developing trainable talents and abilities. This development may require a considerable commitment of time and effort. In the long run, however, adjusting talent can have the same "compounding" effect in improving performance; small increases can lead to appreciable gains. For example, fine-tuning an exercise program can improve the efficiency of workouts, so that no effort is wasted, and no time is lost to injuries due to overexertion.

4. Work Harder and Smarter (Quantity and Quality)

A final strategy is to work harder and to work smarter—to increase the quantity of your work and modify its quality. Combining the two approaches makes it possible to supplement the longer-term improvements of training and development with the more immediate benefits of increased effort.

A commitment to daily exercises that are carefully designed to build endurance, strength, and flexibility is likely to produce better results than increasing just the quantity, or just the quality, of your workouts.

Which Strategy Should You Use?

A simple analysis is possible; ask yourself these four questions:

1. DO I WANT TO WORK MORE CONSISTENTLY?
2. DO I WANT TO WORK HARDER?
3. DO I WANT TO WORK SMARTER?
4. DO I WANT TO WORK HARDER AND SMARTER?

The answer "Yes" to any of these questions provides the starting point. If you say "Yes" to the first question, the next step is to assess your current performance, and decide how it can be adjusted. Exercising every second day, rather than three times a week, for example, requires only a modest amount of time—but the increased consistency is likely to produce noticeable benefits. In sales, working more consistently might mean making the same number of calls *every day*—not just on the days you feel like it—or working just as hard on Wednesday as you do on Monday and Tuesday, even when you have already had your best week in months.

If you answer "Yes" to the second question, you must begin by identifying the controllables and deciding how much more effort you can make. This second option is more demanding than the first, but it is still quite straightforward: you will continue to do the same things, but apply a higher level of effort. If exercising, for example, you would need only to lengthen each workout or increase its intensity; it would not be necessary to add any new activities to the routine. In sales, working harder might mean longer hours, or making more calls than usual on a given day.

The third question takes you further, since "working smarter" inevitably requires that you change your activities and procedures. Once again, it is essential to identify the controllables, but this time it is necessary to adjust the way you control them. For example, to develop respiratory fitness more quickly, and with less risk of injury, you might switch from running to swimming—a change that affects the quality of your effort, and which may very well require the development of new skills or abilities. In sales, working smarter might involve market analysis and strategic planning, so that your calls could be targeted more effectively, with a focus on higher-value customers.

Answering "Yes" to the fourth question suggests that you need to balance the long-term gains of skills development with the more direct, immediate gains that are offered by increased effort. An approach that involves adjustments to both the quality and the quantity of effort takes the longest view of any of the four strategies—and it may have the greatest potential for long-term returns. Just working smarter—and in this way boosting the returns on your investment of effort—may seem the most appealing and efficient option, but it is worth noting that the best performers typically upgrade their skills and seek out opportunities for growth. In the sales world, these top performers are always trying to improve their effectiveness, act more consistently, and, some days, just work harder.

Improved Performance through Self-Management

When results exceed objectives, many people consider that there is no problem—and no occasion for analysis. But when results fall short of objectives, people are quick to ask, "Why?

What happened? Who is to blame? What do I do?" Self-managers rephrase this question: "What can *I* do?" If others judge that you have failed, it sometimes seems that the only solution is to stop doing what you are doing—to succeed by doing something altogether different. By contrast—and by definition—self-managers work with what they've got—themselves. They rely on their genuine capabilities and strengths. They identify what they do well and then identify ways in which to increase the quantity and quality of what they do. Self-managers are constantly aware of how their talent, effort, and opportunity determine their performance, and so can constantly adjust these elements to improve performance. By focusing on the process of managing effort, as well as the original objectives and the end result, self-managers exercise the responsibility they have taken for performance, and make the most of all that lies within their control.

EXPECTATIONS DETERMINE PERFORMANCE,

AND IT'S SELF-CONFIDENCE

THAT DETERMINES EXPECTATIONS.

PRINCIPLE SEVEN
MANAGE SELF-CONFIDENCE

Achieving Your Potential

Previously, we stressed that expectations determine perform-ance. As a person's level of expectations increases, performance increases. Similarly, when expectations are lowered, perform-ance declines. This principle is familiar to coaches, teachers, parents, and managers. In effect, when you expect the best, you may not get it, but you almost always get something that is *better*. Boosting performance by resetting expectations is, of course, something that we can do for ourselves. We needn't wait for someone else to expect our best!

Often, however, our expectation levels are determined, at least partially, by others. There is nothing intrinsically wrong with this. Self-managers constantly "negotiate" with other people over expectations, finding ways to match internal motivations and reinforcements with external demands and rewards. But some people don't negotiate; they let other people set *all* the performance expectations. They do so, sometimes because of conditioning, and sometimes because of a crucial lack of self-confidence.

With sufficient self-confidence, people can achieve their full potential. When our self-confidence is high, we expect more of ourselves, and we perform better. Classic underachievers, how-ever, typically have low levels of self-confidence, and, as a result, they set easily attainable goals and expectations, never "raising the bar" or extending their ambitions.

Figure 7.1
Relationship among Self-Confidence, Expectations, and Performance

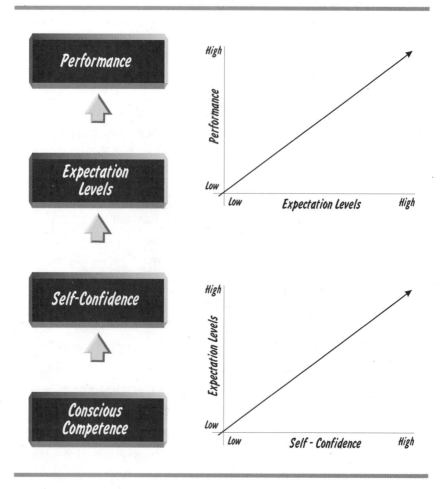

Expectations determine levels of performance, and self-confidence determines levels of expectation. With self-confidence, the basic expectation is "I can do it," whereas without self-confidence, every effort is approached with the basic attitude that "I don't know if I can do it"—or, even worse, "I think I can't do it."

Confidence and Conditioning

What causes a lack of self-confidence? In the first place, it may never be very highly developed. Our early conditioning and upbringing tend to interfere with the growth and the expression of self-confidence. We are taught very early in life not to make positive public statements about ourselves. Parents and teachers tell us not to boast, not to draw attention to our advantages over others. Coaches and managers curb individuals whose expressions of self-regard seem to threaten the unity of the team or the group. We learn very clearly that self-praise is rude, aggressive, thoughtless of others' feelings, and counterproductive.

As a result, healthy self-confidence is often ignored or negatively reinforced and, sometimes, in the long run, extinguished. So it seems that healthy self-confidence can only be expressed privately, or in complex, indirect ways—or else it will be misinterpreted as arrogance. This is a mistaken belief, however. Frank expressions of self-confidence actually make us attractive—to those who are dependent on us, of course, but also to those who are self-managers, and whose own self-assurance allows them to accept positive self-confidence in others. Generally speaking, however, other people will not welcome explicit, self-confident assertions.

Self-confidence, difficult to develop in the first place, is often undermined by our early conditioning. We are taught that it is quite acceptable, and in some cases actually desirable, to make negative or self-doubting statements about ourselves, and to dwell on our errors, shortcomings, and weaknesses. Self-disparagement is encouraged by our instructors and welcomed by our peers, who would much rather hear us express self-doubts than self-praise. Positive statements about ourselves and our performance are likely to be perceived as "bragging" and self-serving. But we can usually count on a sympathetic hearing when we criticize ourselves. Consider, for example, that one of the best ways to discourage other people's interest in you is to answer the question "How are you?" in a positive way: "Great! Finished up all my paperwork this morning, and I've cleared a solid afternoon to work on my next two proposals." "Yeah. Well, I'm off; see you later." Compare the response you get when your answer is negative: "Oh—well, I just managed to catch up with my paperwork, and already I'm up to my neck in these proposals—haven't even started them yet, and the morning's already shot..." "I know what you mean—where does the day go? Those proposals take forever. Why don't we grab a coffee...."

Those negative responses do invite more sympathy, more camaraderie, and a considerable amount of attention. But in the long run, negative self-criticism reinforces the self-doubts that you express, and strengthens the habit of making self-deprecating statements.

Self-confidence, then, is easily undermined, even when it does manage to develop, since it barely has any public existence. Instead, we build up a daily public discourse about our faults and the things that have gone wrong. These public statements inevitably become private statements—the sort of remark we make to ourselves—and can drive out even our private, internal sense of confidence. Psychologists have said that any external comment a person makes has usually been stated 99 times internally.

The Disappearance of Achievements

When self-confidence is not promoted, it is difficult to sustain. When self-doubt is encouraged, it easily establishes itself as the norm. In effect, we are taught not to take much notice of our everyday accomplishments. We don't *describe* them as being very special, so no one else *perceives* them as special. Consequently, no one values our achievements very highly. We may finally stop paying any serious attention to the things that we really do well. Consider the way most people, when asked what sort of day they have had, focus on things that went wrong, things they didn't do well, and things that didn't get done. A teacher, for instance, will only remember the student who didn't seem to get the point, and forget the other twenty-nine who did. Or a manager will focus on his poor performers, neglecting to consider the majority of employees who are getting on with the job.

The typically negative accounts we give of our days needn't be entirely despairing. A good sense of what remains undone, what has to be improved, or what needs adjustment is often a valuable source of new initiatives. When we know what is going wrong, we can begin to try to set things right. But learning from our mistakes in this way is limited. It cultivates conscious incompetence—a clear awareness of our inabilities—and can lead to unconscious competence.

The Self-Confidence Model

Obviously, those who develop only their conscious incompetence are likely to lack self-confidence. Everything they learn confirms and elaborates their low self-estimation.

Self-doubters generalize about themselves on the basis of conscious incompetence. They can see only their weaknesses and failings, and they take these shortcomings to represent the limits of their ability. As a result, their self-evaluations are typically "all-or-nothing" judgments: "I didn't close that sale today; I can't sell anything!"

All-or-nothing generalizations on the basis of conscious competence, however, are just as risky: "I made a sale today; I must be a great salesperson!" Those who focus exclusively on the positive, and learn only from what they do well, do develop a fuller sense of their strengths. They can do what they do well consistently: they cultivate conscious competence, and, on this basis, a form of self-confidence can be developed. However, self-confidence grounded in conscious competence alone is limited, and peculiarly vulnerable. Its value is offset by unconscious incompetence: people who do not know when they perform poorly cannot really begin to identify growth opportunities or develop new abilities.

Figure 7.2
Self-Confidence Model

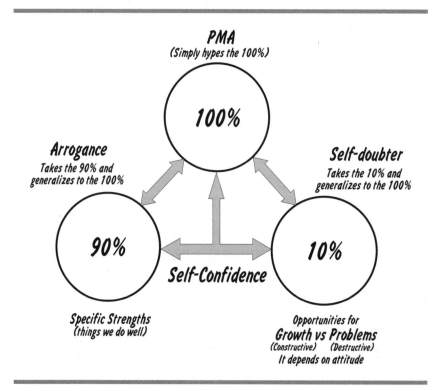

Those who are aware of their strengths and achievements are far more confident—and may be too confident, in fact. Arrogant people understand what they *have done* as the limit to what they (or anyone else) *can do*. They simply do not recognize opportunities for growth and development. Unless this conscious incompetence is developed, a person will continue to deal with problems *as problems*, rather than recognizing them as opportunities for growth. Genuine success is more than just solving the same problems again and again—it involves self-development, and taking on new challenges.

Figure 7.3
Self-Analysis to Maximize Performance

Aspects I Do Well	*Opportunities for Growth*
_____	_____
_____	_____
_____	_____
_____	_____
_____	_____

Self-Management Model to Maximize Performance
Maximum Performance = Repeating the strengths 90% + Opportunity for Growth
Minimum Performance = Repeating the 10%

The best foundation for self-confidence, then, is the fullest learning process, in which we recognize, and learn from, both what we do well and what we do not do well. When conscious competence is balanced by conscious incompetence, it is possible to build on a time-tested foundation of strengths and reliable talents, while seeking growth opportunities in areas where we are not yet fully competent. A self-confident person avoids the extreme generalizations of self-doubt and arrogance, consciously balancing an awareness of strengths and an awareness of potential. A *problem* is approached, not as an obstacle, but as an opportunity; an *achievement* is understood, not as an end in itself, but as part of an ongoing process of renewed effort and improvement.

Figure 7.4
Self-Managing Confidence Levels

Two Major Tasks...

I The breaking of bad internal habit patterns such as:	Self-Management
1. Ignoring positive performance.	10%
2. Misinterpreting performance that is moving in a negative direction.	Don't
3. The energetic reliving of a negative again, and again, and again.......	(Extinction)

II The building of GOOD internal habit patterns such as:	Self-Management
1. Recognizing positive performance and qualities.	90%
2. Dwelling on achievements.	Do !
3. The energetic reliving or rehearsal of a positive event.	(Development)

Building Self-Confidence for Self-Management

In this context, as in others, self-management requires reconditioning and the formation of new habits. Building self-confidence involves, first, breaking old habit patterns. These patterns include

- ignoring one's positive accomplishments
- misrepresenting performance by describing it in negative terms
- devoting energy to reliving negative events again and again
- deflecting others' compliments with self-disparagement

As well, new habit patterns must be established.

- RECOGNIZE YOUR POSITIVE PERFORMANCES AND GOOD QUALITIES—AND EXPRESS THEM

- DWELL ON ACHIEVEMENTS AND REINFORCE THEM

- DEVOTE ENERGY TO RELIVING OR REHEARSING POSITIVE EVENTS

- REINFORCE OTHERS' POSITIVE RESPONSES TO YOUR ACCOMPLISHMENTS

Techniques for Building Self-Confidence

Direct, practical techniques may be used to assist in this process of reconditioning. Here are just a few.

1. Promote the Complimenter (But Not the Flatterer)

A crucial step in building self-confidence is to learn to compliment oneself. Note that compliments are not to be equated with flattery. Flattery always generalizes, and so exaggerates, a person's good performance or positive qualities—"You're the greatest golfer I know! Everyone thinks so!"

Figure 7.5
Learn to Compliment Yourself

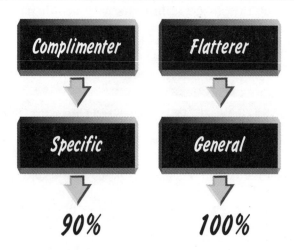

Review your accomplishments on a daily basis, perhaps even dwell on them.

There is plenty of flattery out there in the world. Genuine *compliments*, however, are rarer—and therefore more valuable—since they are specific and concrete. Compliments don't make absolute claims, but they do make accurate claims— "That's the best approach shot you've made today!"

It's nice to receive compliments. For self-confidence, however, it's more important to be able to compliment yourself. This involves reviewing and rehearsing your accomplishments on a daily basis, identifying the things you do well and rewarding yourself for them. This sort of internal reinforcement boosts performance. But take care to assess your successes objectively, rather than reinforcing them indiscriminately. Effort should be rewarded; so should effectiveness. But non-effort should never be rewarded, even if it is associated with startlingly good results.

2. Silence the Critic

It's fine to learn from your mistakes, but only once. We tend to relive failures and errors again and again, but there's no new learning to be acquired in this way. Rather, it is important to become aware of this tendency, and the self-criticism that goes along with it. Self-doubting and defeatist statements don't really provide much emotional relief, and they can damage your performance. When an error occurs, you can learn from it *once*, and *move on*, avoiding a recurrence in the future.

Figure 7.6
Silence the Critic

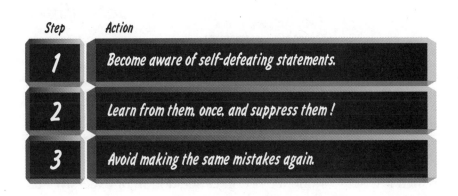

Step	Action
1	Become aware of self-defeating statements.
2	Learn from them, once, and suppress them!
3	Avoid making the same mistakes again.

Going forward, there is more to be learned, and more confidence to be gained, from reliving your past successes or rehearsing for future successes. Such rehearsals, in particular, not only displace self-criticism, but provide an effective way to set positive expectations.

3. The Self-Confidence Continuum

Self-confidence occupies a middle ground between self-doubt and arrogance.

Figure 7.7
The Self-Confidence Continuum

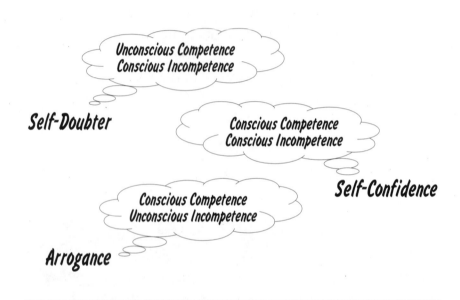

This is a genuine continuum: there is no distinct point at which low self-confidence becomes self-doubt, or excessive self-confidence becomes outright arrogance. We move back and forth along this continuum every day. As a result, healthy self-confidence must be developed and constantly sustained against the tensions exerted by both extremes. The key to this ongoing negotiation is action. Continually renewing your efforts allows you to dispel anxiety and doubts, and, at the same time, to test the limits that arrogance pretends to ignore.

A CTION

A BSORBS

A NXIETY

4. Learn to Accept Compliments

One of the quickest ways to diminish self-confidence is also one of our most common tendencies: to deflect a compliment with a "Yes, but...." Conditioning makes it difficult for us to accept compliments, so, rather than let them stand, we tack on a negative rider: "That's the best approach shot you've made all day!" "Yes, but my putting is falling to pieces." The "Yes, but..." functions, ostensibly, as modest good manners—although it is actually an unnecessary self-criticism, and even something of an insult. To set aside a compliment in this way is, in effect, to tell others that they are mistaken, wrong, or unperceptive, and that they should not have recognized your accomplishment.

In fact, what may be intended as a modest consideration for other people's feelings can, in the long run, come back to hurt your own. Consider the executive who made a lively, effective presentation to his board of directors. When congratulated on his work, he politely turned aside the compliments, and added that, actually, he hadn't been able to get through all his material. That evaluation spread through the room, and through the organization, so that by the time he returned to his office, it was common knowledge that he had made a mess of his presentation—and his immediate superiors wanted to know why.

Good manners, as well as good self-management, actually require us to accept and confirm compliments. At the very least, "Yes, but..." should be replaced by "Yes—thanks!" The compliment—and your accomplishment—should be registered, not set aside.

REPLACE "YES, BUT"

WITH "YES, THANKS."

In turn, "Yes—thanks!" should give way to "Yes—I appreciate that!" And finally, "Yes—I appreciate that!" should be replaced by a "Yes, and..." Rather than deflect a compliment, a self-confident person adds on to it, corroborating the positive public statements other people make. The most confident people promote themselves—without self-aggrandizement—by carrying the compliment a little farther: "Yes, I've adjusted my stance, and it's helping."

REPLACE "YES, BUT"

WITH "YES, AND...."

The "Yes, and..." approach allows the expression, and so the internal reinforcement, of your self-confidence. So, for example, a student could respond to praise by saying, "Yes, and I am trying to make the same effort in other subjects." This sort of self-promotion works internally and externally. It expresses an internal commitment, and makes it public, directing others' attention to the results you plan to achieve. The "promotion" can also be extended to others. Consider the high-scoring athlete who says, "Thank you—I felt strong out there, and the whole team was playing well too."

5. Report, Don't Judge

Statements about oneself, whether private or public, and positive or negative, need to be strictly controlled, if self-confidence is to be sustained. Reporting, not judging, helps conserve confidence; it also helps control arrogance.

Figure 7.8
Reporting vs Judging

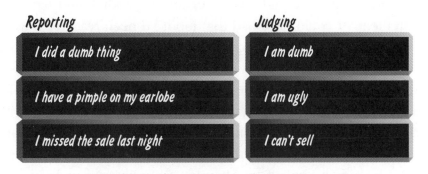

Reporting	Judging
I did a dumb thing	I am dumb
I have a pimple on my earlobe	I am ugly
I missed the sale last night	I can't sell

Reporting is a way of effectively learning from mistakes.
Judging is a way of effectively destroying self-confidence.
Arrogance, as opposed to self-confidence, is embellishing the positives.

An objective, concise description of an achievement is more useful, in the long run, than an exaggerated evaluation. "I scored a goal this game" is sufficient grounds for self-reinforcement;

the judgment that "I am the best goal scorer on the team" is likely to push a person along the confidence continuum towards arrogance.

When negative circumstances or events must be described, it is important to confine oneself to a simple report, as opposed to a critical judgment. It is enough to say, for instance, "I didn't make the sale yesterday"; self-confidence will be undermined if you go on to add a judgment such as "Therefore, I can't sell." Reporting is an effective way of identifying and learning from mistakes: "I didn't score a goal this game." Judging offsets anything gained in the experience by diminishing self-confidence: "I can't score any more."

6. Learn to Deal with Criticism

Other people will often attempt, either consciously or unconsciously, to erode our self-confidence. Typically, this will take the form of an "I could have..." or an "Anybody could have..." statement: "I could have had that job if I'd been ready to move to the suburbs"; "Anybody could have passed that test (after all, you did)." People say things like this to protect their own egos, and to compensate for their own lack of genuine self-confidence. They see something about you that they lack, and take a cheap shot to make up for it. As a rule, cheap shots are aimed at those who have or do something special. In a way, then, you can take them as a kind of backhanded compliment—or you can learn to self-manage them.

There are three ways to manage criticism:

(a) Absolute Acceptance or Rejection

The quickest and the simplest is just to agree: "That's a godawful tie to wear to an important meeting." "Yes, I guess it is." You can save energy by merely assenting to the criticism; there's little or no engagement, and the episode is soon over. And, when you keep on doing what you are doing, you will make it clear how little you value the person's opinion.

(b) Confrontation

An alternative, rather more demanding, is to counterattack: "Is that what you're wearing to the presentation?" "Yes it is—and look who's talking: where'd you get those high-tide pants, anyway?" This is probably the least effective way to deal with criticism, since it is likely to escalate the unfriendly exchange. It also suggests that the criticism got to you—or else you wouldn't be responding in kind.

(c) Seek Clarification

A third option, and perhaps the most effective and productive, is to "deflect the question": "Some swing—no-one would ever know you'd been taking golf lessons." "I have been working hard with the pro—what do *you* think I should be doing?" A response like this is a quick way of finding out whether or not there is some genuinely constructive criticism. And it usually stems negative criticism: nothing is more flattering to a person than being asked for an opinion, especially if the opinion is taken seriously.

7. Develop "Self-Marketing" Tools

"Self-talk"—telling yourself and others about yourself, your abilities, and your potential—is one of the principal self-marketing tools used to build self-confidence. It can take many forms on many occasions. One useful exercise is interviewing yourself: imagine that you are making a presentation to a supervisor, coach, teacher, or peer who has asked you to describe yourself, your accomplishments, and your goals and objectives. Interviews like this can be made the basis of a "mental scorecard": keep track of your progress, and update your presentation.

Another useful marketing tool is *reputation*: every successful person, organization, and system has one. By creating an image of yourself and your activities, you can establish expectations, and create the conditions in which you can have conspicuous success. There are many ways to develop an image, from simple externals—taking care to look good, well-dressed, and neat—to more complex methods of "self-advertisement." For instance, a careful refusal to participate in "ain't it awful" sessions will, in the long run, build up your image as the kind of person for whom things simply "ain't awful." Like self-deprecating statements, endless rehashings of what has gone wrong tend to obscure everything that has gone well. It's much better to take a vigorous positive approach, and be the one who starts the discussion about how to improve the situation.

8. Keep an Eye on Your Benchmarks

Remember, self-confidence consists in a balanced awareness of ability and potential, of what you do well and what you can do better. As you build self-confidence, it's important to have realistic reference points. No matter how well you do something, you will always be able to find someone who might do it better or faster. Your achievements, quite rightly, are the evidence of your success—but there is always room to improve.

Confidence and the Self-Manager

Self-managers, because they cultivate conscious competence and conscious incompetence, have high levels of self-confidence. Self-managers compound their effectiveness by building on strengths and by developing new skills. Even quite small but well-executed improvements can, over the long term, improve performance significantly. Conscious competence gives self-managers a stable foundation for their confidence, and allows them to approach incompetence as an opportunity. Conscious incompetence, at the same time, allows for continual growth and development, and ensures a kind of realism in forming objectives and plans. Self-managers feel confident—but they don't think they are perfect, so they can perceive areas for personal and professional improvement as opportunities, not inadequacies.

CHANGE "I SHOULD" TO "I WILL,"

AND SET A TIMETABLE.

PRINCIPLE EIGHT
COMMIT YOURSELF

Commitment vs "Commitments"

Busy people often speak of "having a lot of commitments"—places to go, people to see, things to do. There is an important distinction, however, between "commitments" like these, which are typically external requirements and demands, and *commitment* itself, which is an internal process.

"COMMITMENTS" WORK FROM THE OUTSIDE IN;

COMMITMENT WORKS FROM THE INSIDE OUT.

Commitment is self-initiated. Making a genuine commitment involves an internal dedication of our effort towards some goal. Although such a commitment can be expressed, announced, and made public, it is uniquely private and personal. Strictly speaking, each of us makes our own commitments—no one else can make them for us.

When we refer to our commitments, then, it is important to distinguish between the genuine commitments—the "will do" commitments—that we initiate ourselves and "commitments" in a looser sense—the "should do" tasks, duties, and obligations that are imposed on us by others. Of course, an imposed obligation or assignment can be treated as a genuine commitment. That is, *we* can *choose* to dedicate our effort to an objective that someone else—a teacher, employer, or a companion—

proposes. We can internalize the external demand, converting it from a "should do" to a "will do."

But the essential distinction remains. The difference is easy to observe in people's performance. Consider the difference between a person who makes and keeps a commitment and a person who is "just doing the job." When goals are imposed, and are not internalized, the level of commitment is never very high. When we pursue a goal that someone else has set for us, we tend to require continual external reinforcements, and we can look forward at best to a hollow satisfaction. Externally imposed duties and obligations depend on an external structure, and the loss of that structure usually puts an end to effort. (No one keeps doing homework, for instance, after they leave school!) A real commitment, however, keeps going even if external structures and props disappear.

Commitment and Performance

Commitment is crucial to performance. The most successful parents, teachers, coaches, and managers know this. They have learned not to impose goals or objectives on others; instead, they work as facilitators or catalysts, encouraging others to set their own objectives. They *ask* others what they want to accomplish, rather than telling them what they want or should want, knowing that the only truly effective goals are those that are self-selected. Your own goals have real meaning for you.

In the commitment process, people move towards a decision on what *will* be done; through active involvement and personal participation, they commit themselves to specific efforts. When people are excluded from the decision-making process, and are merely presented with its conclusions, they may very well assent to them. But this only provides an agreement on what *should* be done: there is no commitment to action.

Figure 8.1
Commitment Process

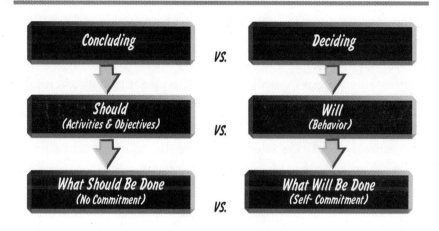

Concluding	VS.	Deciding
Should (Activities & Objectives)	VS.	Will (Behavior)
What Should Be Done (No Commitment)	VS.	What Will Be Done (Self-Commitment)

Learn to Act, Not Always React!

Decisions and Conclusions

Deciding what *will* be done, rather than *concluding* what *should* be done, is a defining characteristic of a good self-manager. Self-managers make genuine, personal commitments to perform specific activities. These commitments are not to be equated with imposed duties: the self-manager begins with an "I will," not an "I should." "I should" is tantamount to a confession of passivity and inaction; it carries with it the inevitable implication "But I haven't, and maybe I won't." There is really no "I" in "I should." When a smoker says "I should stop smoking," he is simply stating what *everybody* knows; he is not really saying anything about his personal efforts or intentions.

The very common use of "I should" reflects an interesting observation: most people would rather be thought lazy than unintelligent. When people say "I should quit smoking/work harder/exercise more frequently," they show that they *know* what is right, even if they can't (or won't) do it. Typically, an "I should" statement is followed by a "*But...*"—and then any number of excuses and rationalizations for not doing something they know is in their own best interests.

The self-manager's commitment—the "I will"—may also be contrasted to mere compliance. That is, people will often take on an obligation or assignment in a half-hearted way. They begin, not with an "I will," but with an "I will—IF..." This approach reflects fairly explicitly the need for an *external* structure to support the activity. As long as reinforcements are supplied, compliant people will perform the required or desired actions. But their motivation is weak, their attitudes are fragile, and they are easily dissuaded from *persisting*—one of the big "ifs" is usually "if it's easy enough, and nothing goes wrong."

Psychological Time Management

Moving from decision-making to a specific "I will" improves the self-manager's "psychological time management." Generally speaking, *one* decision is worth a hundred *conclusions*—and the amount of time and energy needed to form a hundred conclusions represents a huge waste of resources. A sales rep who wants to improve her performance can come to the conclusion that "I should work harder" again and again—but it doesn't really help. What is needed is a decision: "I will make a minimum of ten calls every day." Self-managers develop decision-making skills and habits, so that they can avoid the "I should" time-and-energy trap. They accept objectives, but they commit to *effort*, which can be managed directly and effectively. (The power of these decisions, and the consequences for time and effort management, are discussed in more detail in the next chapter.)

Self-Commitment

When we think of making genuine commitments, we usually think of the commitments that we make to others. Most of us tend to keep these commitments. After all, we don't want to let people down, we want to appear to be reliable, and we want others' good opinion. All these reasons seem to have to do with what *other people* think and feel. But in fact, at the very foundation of our efforts to keep commitments is an internal *self-commitment*, a response to self-oriented, internal demands. Naturally we want others to have a good opinion of us; at a deeper level, however, we *must* have a good opinion of ourselves.

Selfishness, Self-Commitment, and Selflessness

This basic self-commitment is not always considered directly. Other people pat us on the back for keeping our commitments to them, but we seldom congratulate ourselves for keeping a self-commitment. As with self-confidence, our conditioning often interferes with self-commitment. We are taught that it is good to be committed to other people, but that it is selfish to be committed to ourselves. There is a considerable difference, however, between self-commitment and selfishness.

Selfish people only keep commitments to themselves, to the exclusion of all other commitments. Their attitude is, basically, "I am all that matters." At the opposite extreme, selfless people only keep commitments to other people, taking the view that "I'm doing it for them." Both extremes are unhealthy. Too little self-regard is just as damaging as too much. Self-commitment, as a middle ground between the two, balances the claims of the self and others. Self-committed people keep important commitments to themselves and to others. Their attitude is that "When I win, we all win—and when we all win, I win too."

Figure 8.2
The Self-Commitment Race Track

Selfishness

Only keeps commitments
to self to the exclusion
of all the other commitments
(I am all that matters)

Self-Commitment

Keeps self-commitments and
other important commitments
-job, family (When I win, we
all win)

Selflessness

Only keeps outside
commitments (I'm
doing it for them)

Conditioning and Commitment

Our conditioning also leads us to expect and respond to external controls. In every setting, we find authority figures urging us to do things, not for ourselves, but for others. Parents coax, "Please, do it for me"; teachers promise, "If you do it, I will..."; coaches implore, "One for the Gipper"; and managers level with us, "My job is on the line." Most of our early experiences are of coaxing, not coaching: other people cajole, coax, and reward us for cooperating with them to achieve their objectives. As long as the external controls are maintained, there is always motivation for us to do the things other people want done. But when the external controls disappear, so do the motivation and commitment.

Unfortunately, the *removal* of these external controls is also a common feature of our upbringing. That is, as we mature, parents and teachers begin to take away, or significantly reduce, these controls, expecting that we will internalize the reinforcement process, becoming *internally* motivated and self-controlled. Their hopes are not always realized, as many people continue to require external direction and external reinforcement to function effectively.

As a result, people lack, or lose, self-commitment, because it is easier and, superficially, more rewarding to respond to external direction and reinforcement than to internal, self-imposed (and perhaps more rigorous) demands. When we leave it up to other people to decide what we should do, their demands are often less taxing and more precisely defined than the requirements we would make for ourselves. Like self-confidence, self-commitment is something that must be developed and reinforced. And no one else can do it for us: we must do it for ourselves.

Developing Self-Commitment: Practical Techniques

1. Recognize Your Self-Commitments

Learn to recognize—and reinforce—the distinction between selfishness and self-commitment in all your activities. It's important to take credit for self-commitment, rather than to discount it as self-interest or self-centredness. Think of it in relation to all the other behaviors that we value highly. Everyone knows, for instance, that it is important to keep promises: self-commitment is, quite simply, keeping promises to oneself and to others. This positive, productive characteristic can be seen in all the things we do to help ourselves and to help others. Even when the results do not turn out as we wish, the basic commitment remains as a source of legitimate pride.

2. Don't Take Yourself for Granted

As a result of our conditioning and our typical social practices, we tend to pay the least attention to the people we take for granted—the people closest to us. We are often more likely to offer high levels of commitment, if only on a short-term basis, to acquaintances or neighbours than to oblige closer friends or even family members. Consider the motorist who gladly disrupts his own plans to help another motorist stranded on the highway, or the good neighbour who will drop whatever he is doing at home to fix a neighbour's leaky faucet.

Most people who agree to meet a friend to go jogging on a Saturday morning will be there, no matter what. Why? They have made a commitment to the friend, and there is some risk in failing to keep to commitment—not the least of which is the risk of damaging their reputation. If the friend calls Friday night to cancel, many people would use the cancellation as an excuse to skip jogging the next day. But who is the exercise for? If you fail to keep a commitment to yourself, the failure is not public. No-one else knows about it. But there is still a substantial risk to your reputation—that is, to your opinion of yourself.

The closer we are to people, the more easily we take them for granted—and, typically, the less we may offer in terms of response, feedback, and commitments of energy. It is often difficult to recognize that we take ourselves for granted in this way. But no one is closer to you than yourself. An effort must be made, then, to establish the basic self-commitment that is essential to good performance and results. Since your own opinion of yourself is really much more important than others' opinions, it is good to be aware that making and keeping commitments to yourself is one of the best things you can do to promote self-esteem.

3. Develop a Balance in Your Life and Career

Self-managers manage the internal components of performance, rather than allowing themselves to managed by externals. As a result, they can balance the different aspects of their lives and careers, by considering their investments of energy and the returns they receive. Consider "time management," for example. Conventionally, "time management" consists of being managed by time: our priorities are directly related to, and even determined by, the amount of time we spend on different activities.

Figure 8.3
Self-Managing a Balanced Lifestyle

Commitment Area	% of Time	Priority	
		Traditional	Self-Management
Job and/or Career	80%	1	1
Family and/or Friends	15%	2	1
Self	5%	3	1

Typically, people rank their commitments according to the amount of time they spend on them—and, almost without exception, they rank themselves last. Self-managers, however, assess their commitments. Their essential commitments are all number-one priorities; the self-manager is concerned in every area to maximize returns on energy.

4. Choose Your Own Shoulds

It's better to make a decision—an "I will"—than to accept all the "shoulds" that others are only too willing to impose upon you. After all, some of them are "garbage shoulds," as opposed to the necessary "shoulds"—the ones you have to negotiate in order to continue creating your opportunities for success. Self-managers analyze each situation, separating out irrelevant or trivial claims, and focus on the factors that they can control, so as to commit themselves to action. In this way, they set and achieve *their own* objectives, and they enjoy the satisfaction and confidence that consistently good performance provides.

Figure 8.4
The Effects of "Garbage Shoulds"

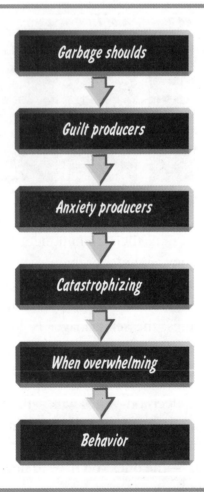

Reacting to "shoulds"—the dictates of other people's value systems, their opinions, or their exemplary behavior—is not as likely to lead to accomplishments. In fact, "I should..." typically leads to an "I should have..."—and ultimately to an "I could have, but...." Unlike an "I will," an "I should" continually uses up energy, without producing results. It easily slips into retrospective rationalizations and self-defensive excuses. And in the process, these "shoulds" can produce guilt, anxiety, and various crisis-ridden attempts to compensate for poor performance.

Even when the "should" is so compelling that we must finally satisfy its demands, a great deal of energy and emotion may be wasted in reaching the objective. Decisions that determine actions lead more directly and efficiently to successful accomplishments.

CHANGE "I SHOULD" TO "I WILL"

AND SET A TIMETABLE

Self-managers change "shoulds" and "coulds" to the active statement "I will"—a statement that, unlike "I should" or "I could," expresses the expectations that determine performance. Self-managers must sometimes obey "shoulds" that are imposed by others. But they do not simply accept the "shoulds" as conclusions; they incorporate them in their own thinking and behavior as decisions that lead to specific consequences in the future.

5. Stand Back
Give yourself the benefit of your own good advice, and have the

good sense to take the advice offered. This is part of paying more attention to the person closest to you—yourself.

Many people "know better than they do": that is, while they can provide good advice to others, they don't seem to manage their own situations very well. This has to do with our customary tendency to take ourselves for granted: we give our best insights and strategies to others, but don't consider ourselves important enough to deserve the same support.

A quick way to overcome this tendency is to offer yourself the same concern and consideration you would a friend or family member. Consider what you would recommend to another person in your situation. What advice would you give? What strategies would you recommend? How would you motivate and encourage the person? Such an approach distances you from the immediate anxieties and emotions of your situation, allowing you to see more clearly what actions are needed, and which actions will lead most directly to your goals. In a challenging situation, it's often easier to think of reasons not to do things than it is to think of reasons to act. Giving yourself advice is a good way to think positively, constructively, and realistically. We usually expect a lot of ourselves; sometimes, we expect just too much. But when we advise others, we are likely to set more reasonable objectives, or to suggest a gradual development. You can and should give yourself the benefit of that moderation.

6. Avoid Over-Analyzing

Analysis and decision-making are crucial activities—as long as they are projected towards the future. It's important to start from where you are now, and to move forward, rather than be pulled backward. People sometimes use so much energy in reassessing and reevaluating past events that little is left over for the present and the future. It's a good idea to learn from the past, but only once. Too much analysis of what has already happened can produce anxiety, guilt, irresolution, and indecisiveness. You can choose where to direct your energy: the future or the past. By focusing on the future, you can begin to pursue objectives by managing effort, rather than be pushed along by the past and its circumstances.

PUT YOUR ENERGY INTO DOING IT,

NOT

INTO THINKING YOU SHOULD DO IT.

PRINCIPLE NINE
DECIDE ONCE:
PSYCHOLOGICAL TIME MANAGEMENT

Time Management

"Time management" is usually offered as a means for people to take control of their lives, to improve their performance, or to increase their efficiency and satisfaction. In practice, however, "time management" often becomes "management by time": people come to be managed by their schedules and timetables, rather than using these tools to facilitate their progress towards objectives.

As we have already noted, this is because time is an objective, external measure of the *duration*, but not the *intensity*, of effort. There is no direct, reliable correlation between the amount of time a person spends on an activity and the kind of effort they make. Of course, time has to be allotted for activities, but that is just the beginning of genuinely effective action. Giving yourself an hour every morning to keep up with daily correspondence may be a good idea, but it will succeed only if you bring the required attitude and effort to the daily task. Similarly, if you want to get into shape, it's not enough to spend two hours a day at the gym: you have to work out too.

So long as time management is restricted to scheduling and rescheduling activities, then, it is unlikely to produce any genuine, long-term benefits. Making appointments, allocating blocks of time, writing up "to-do" lists, and setting deadlines gives us the sense that we are in control, but this sort of time management can easily become a defensive or compensatory activity. It is often a *response* to circumstances, a *reaction* to results, rather than a means to choose an action and produce results.

Effective performance requires a "deeper" time management, a management of *psychological time*, to address the effort and energy issues at the heart of performance. The best results are achieved when "psychological time"—the subjective experience of a period during which energy is applied and efforts are sustained—is used to its best advantage. Psychological time management involves allocations of internal resources, rather than scheduling external circumstances, to achieve specific, well-formed objectives.

Decisioning Model

Effective psychological time management is based on the decisioning model that all self-managers follow.

PLANNING: CHOOSE WHAT SHOULD BE DONE.

DECISION: TURN THE "I SHOULD" TO "I WILL."

ACTION: TURN "I WILL" TO "IT'S DONE!"

Each stage of this process has its own special challenges. In the planning stage, for instance, it is important to move towards a decision, rather than be pushed along by a conclusion. In choosing what should be done, it is easy, and often tempting, to let others do the thinking, and supply the "shoulds." However, such "shoulds" are not always the product of very much thinking. Even when a certain course of action is strongly recommended, it should be thought through from your individual perspective. Only in this way can you arrive at a decision, turning "I should" to "I will."

Once a decision has been made, new challenges begin to arise. In turning the "I will" to "It's done," a host of obstacles, both external and internal, may appear. External, circumstantial difficulties may seem more numerous, but it is the internal obstacles that are most serious. The urgency or difficulty of the job at hand, or the effort required to carry out the "I will," may inspire second thoughts and self-doubt. It may be tempting to revisit the decision, to rethink the issue—or to exaggerate the circumstantial difficulties, so as to find reasons not to proceed.

It is at this point that a genuine *decision* provides a reliable foothold. A mere "I should," the product of your own or other people's conclusions, is easily abandoned. But when *you* have made a decision, you have made a personal investment. It's harder to sacrifice, since there is something of your own at stake— your own good idea, and your own good opinion of yourself. Self-managers control self-doubt and resist the influence of second thoughts by sticking to the model: once the decision is made, they buckle down and perform the action. Even if the desired results are not attained—or not attained at once—they have the satisfaction of following through, the feeling of accomplishment.

PERSONAL POWER = KEEPING A COMMITMENT

Sometimes, of course, it's just not possible to turn the "I will" into an "It's done." When this happens, a strong self-manager begins the process again, refusing to get bogged down in remorse, performance anxiety, or guilt. Psychological time is far too valuable to waste in needless retrospection; it is most productively directed to planning, decision-making, and action.

SELF-MANAGERS DO WHAT THEY SAY

THEY ARE GOING TO DO.

Performance Issues

Poor performance, no matter what form it takes, follows from the ineffective management of psychological time. There are four principal ways in which people waste their energy and time, risk burn-out, and fall short of their goals, all related to the phases of the decisioning model.

PSYCHOLOGICAL TIME MANAGEMENT	PSYCHOLOGICAL TIME WASTERS
PLANNING: CHOOSE WHAT SHOULD BE DONE	*CONCLUSION:* ACCEPTING A "SHOULD"
DECISION: "I WILL"	*SECOND THOUGHTS:* REVISITING THE "SHOULD"
ACTION: TURN "I WILL" TO "IT'S DONE"	*INACTION:* "I SHOULD, BUT...."
SATISFACTION: "I COULD DO THAT — SO I CAN DO MORE"	*FRUSTRATION AND GUILT:* REPLAYING THE FAILURE

Effective psychological time management depends on making the right start. If you begin by passively accepting a conclusion about what should be done, rather than making a decision about what you will do, you are much more likely to have second thoughts—and that indecision is likely, in turn, to prevent you from following through with the planned activity. The resulting failure—an occasion for excuses and a source of guilt—undermines confidence and reinforces the passivity that began the process.

"I WILL DO IT TOMORROW" = "I SHOULD"

Planning and Deciding

The foundation of good time management—and of good self-management—is simply stated, but not always easy to achieve: begin by determining *your own* goals and objectives. Other people will be prepared to tell you what you should do; their demands and requirements should not be ignored, but incorporated in your own plan. Starting out with your own choices greatly increases the chance that you will persevere despite momentary doubts and external obstacles, and that you will achieve a success that reinforces your choice.

We all know that planning should precede action. In practice, however, the need for deliberation is often overwhelmed by the force of demands that strike us as so obvious, so natural, so evidently compelling that all we need to do is assent to them. It seems obvious, for example, that getting into shape is a good idea; *of course* we should exercise and watch our diet. There is so much in our society to reinforce these "shoulds" that we may neglect to work out any specific plan to do so. Instead, we may rush straight into action.

But *unplanned* actions in response to a sense of duty, obligation, or necessity are likely to fail. They take two forms: spontaneous, impulsive, and transient gestures (skipping the salad dressing, or choosing a sugar-free soft drink) and spontaneous, impulsive, and perhaps impractical commitments ("From now on, I will spend one hour a day at the gym!"). Impulsive gestures are not consistent enough to provide any accumulated benefits; impulsive commitments, by contrast, impose routines so rigid and demanding that they cannot be consistently followed. When we make inadequate gestures, we let ourselves off too easily. But when we make impractical commitments, we set ourselves tasks we simply can't hope to complete. As a result, we can only say, "I will do it next time," constantly putting off genuine action.

Planning allows us to transform a general "I should" into a *specific* "I will." When we plan, we relate a proposed action to our actual circumstances, abilities, and resources, so as to develop a feasible, worthwhile objective. A genuine *decision* requires planning. Self-managers make such decisions; as a result, they may have to face difficulties, but they are not as likely to revisit the decision, or to waste energy in rethinking and renewing their commitments. They also avoid the opposite extremes of selfishness and self-sacrifice. In responding to claims made upon them, they consider what they can do, formulating feasible, specific objectives and seeking the satisfaction of attaining them.

Unless we make plans and arrive at decisions, we are inviting failure and guilt. If all we do is make inadequate gestures, we will know we aren't doing enough; if we make impossible commitments, we will soon feel that we are falling behind. It is in such situations that conventional "time management" can create the effect of planning, without actually producing any decisions. Time management certainly looks like planning. Consider, for example, a student whose grades are slipping, and whose teachers are telling him that he should work harder. One way to respond to this pressure is to schedule a one-hour review each day. It takes just minutes to make this resolve, and to block out the new plan on a calendar. The exercise can be very reassuring: the student feels he is dealing with the problem, and that he is taking control. But he has not followed the self-management model. Rather than working up to a decision, he is being pushed by conclusions. He is still responding to what other people think he should do and to what *he* thinks he "should" do. He has not really decided what *he* will *do*. To accept the "should" without planning—adjusting the proposed action to the actual circumstances, abilities, and resources— leads to *empty* resolves.

Action

Self-managers decide to perform deliberate, specific actions that, while they address compelling demands, remain consistent with their known abilities and resources. Self-managers have learned that the *adequate* response is the one that will ultimately realize the desired end result by bringing that result a little closer. As a result, self-managers can turn "I will" to "It's done" more easily than those who form impulsive resolutions: they try to do no more than they are able.

As well, they have more energy and resources to bring to bear on making the "I will" into an "It's done." Self-managers make a decision *once*, and stick to it. They don't waste time and energy in rethinking a conclusion. If you have decided to go to the gym every Monday evening, there are sure to be some nights when it will be late, you will feel too tired, or the traffic will be bad. The temptation is to go through the decision process *again*, reviewing all the good reasons for exercise and for a regular workout, and weighing them against the inconvenience and the circumstantial difficulties. No matter how you decide this time round, having to decide again wastes a considerable amount of energy, and may set up a habit of vacillation that will be hard to break. Strong self-management skills, however, ensure that a good decision, once made, is not revisited. If it's Monday, it's just time for the workout.

Note that the self-manager is inflexible about *good* decisions. Unplanned, spontaneous reactions to a "should" are usually not "good." They are characteristically expressed in *absolute* terms: "I should stop smoking—so that's it, I'll never put one in my mouth again! As of here and now, I've quit!" Unconditional resolutions like this typically make unrealistic demands. As a result, they are likely to be revisited: "But if it's so hard, maybe it *wasn't* such a good idea." Without the mediation of a genuine, personal decision, the conflict between the general "should" and the individual "but" produces a futile vacillation: "I know I should stop smoking—but it's hard—but I should—but...." People in such situations "know better than they do"—and accordingly suffer guilt, lose confidence, and becomes less and less able to face the demands they still acknowledge.

Satisfaction

Perhaps the most damaging effect of hasty, unrealistic resolutions is the deep sense of inability they foster. Unconditional resolutions are usually impossible to fulfil. And a failure to perform some objective expressed in absolute terms may be taken as an *absolute* failure: "I should," when it is followed by "I couldn't," leads irresistibly to "I can't" and, finally, "I won't ever."

The self-manager's feasible, deliberate objectives *can* be achieved. This accomplishment produces only a *relative* satisfaction—but this limitation is crucial to the dynamics of self-management. It has been said that the best thing you can do for yourself and your self-esteem is to make a commitment and keep it (and that the worst thing you can do is make a commitment and not keep it). By planning, deciding, and acting, self-managers take pleasure in achieving as much as they do, while remaining aware that there is more that must (and can) be achieved. This combination of reinforcement and motivation drives a continuous process of accomplishment and new initiative. For the self-manager, turning "I will" into "It's done" is not the *end* of a linear sequence. "It's done" leads naturally to the question, "What's next?": the pleasure of achievement is a moment in a continuous cycle.

YOU ALREADY

HAVE THE POWER

TO CHOOSE—

AND THE

POWER TO CHANGE

CONCLUSION
APPLYING THE PRINCIPLES OF SELF-MANAGEMENT

Overview

The principles of self-management are simple; many of them seem familiar, even self-evident. As noted in the introduction, however, the challenge is not to assent to these principles but to *apply* them consistently and effectively. As we have suggested, there are many sources of resistance to self-management, both in the outside world and in the conditioned individual. Perhaps the most basic challenge for the self-manager is to manage *from the inside out*: to reclaim one's individuality as the source of motivation, reinforcement, and authority. The nine principles set out in the preceding chapters are indeed familiar from our experience in managing, or being managed by, others—but they become fresh and powerful when we take them as the basis for managing *ourselves*.

UNDERSTAND PERFORMANCE—THE KEY TO SUCCESS.

YOU ARE *ACCOUNTABLE* FOR YOUR RESULTS,

BUT

YOU ARE *RESPONSIBLE* FOR YOUR PERFORMANCE.

The first step in reclaiming internal motivation and reinforcement is to recognize the area of endeavour that we can fully control—performance. The results that others judge us by are *all that they can see* of what we do. When we share their evaluations, taking external results as our only basis for self-evaluation and self-understanding, we ignore the efforts we know we make, and have no way to appraise what we *do*, as opposed to what others see us as having done. The self-manager's recognition of his or her performance as the means to achieve (and to improve) results opens up the "self" that is managed.

EXPECTATIONS DICTATE PERFORMANCE.

IF YOU THINK YOU CAN—

OR THINK YOU CAN'T—

YOU'RE RIGHT.

We take this proposition for granted in dealing with other people—so much so that, in return, we allow others to set expectations for us. Self-management depends upon resisting this imposition, and setting expectations for ourselves. In this way, we define for ourselves what we will do, and we communicate to others the criteria by which our actions should be judged, tapping the power of the self-fulfilling prophecy.

Setting expectations, however, is not just a matter of choosing an arbitrary goal. Expectations should be *managed:* the point is to set goals that are worthwhile and feasible. Self-managers do this by considering both their current performance and the desired results, so as to set an ideal "incentive gap"—one that represents a significant improvement in performance, but which also lies within the self-manager's abilities. By creating a *series* of well-defined successes, rather than striving for a single, distant objective, the self-manager develops a continuous process of challenge and achievement that is driven by self-reinforcement.

REINFORCEMENT CREATES HABITS.

YOU ONLY *HAVE* TO DO IT

UNTIL YOU WANT TO DO IT;

THEN YOU DON'T *HAVE* TO DO IT

ANY MORE.

Our earliest learning experiences predominantly consist of negative reinforcement and the extinction of behaviors. The structures of family, school, and social institutions sustain this repressive function, while selectively encouraging specific behaviors through positive reinforcement. We learn, as a result, to expect all reinforcements to come from other people. By internalizing the role of reinforcement, however, self-managers reduce the damaging effects of negative reinforcement from without, and take advantage of the constructive power of positive reinforcement from within. Setting their own expectations, and providing their own rewards, self-managers break free of a dependency on others for both direction and approval. Remember—habits require *internal* reinforcement to become habitual.

MOTIVATE YOURSELF—OTHERS CAN'T.

90% PULL AND 10% PUSH:

THE IDEAL MOTIVATIONAL MIX

As self-determining, self-reinforcing agents, self-managers are put in touch with their internal motivations. Although we often speak of "motivating" other people to act in certain ways, motivations are strictly private. At best, coaches, teachers, and managers can only attempt to provide the kinds of reinforcement that they believe will connect with people's motives. This attempt may always be mistaken: people's motivations are not directly available for our inspection. However, as *self*-managers, we can never be mistaken about our own motivations; as a result, we are always in the best position to "motivate" and reinforce our actions.

MAXIMIZE RETURN ON ENERGY (ROE).

ROE: THREE STEPS

1) ESTABLISH COMMITMENT AREAS.

2) SET PRIORITIES.

3 MANAGE ENERGY WITHIN COMMITMENT AREAS.

It is only natural to seek a good return on our effort. But it is easy to mistake the *time* we spend on an activity for the *effort* we invest. However, when we focus on performance, we can calculate a return on *energy*. External results matter most in other people's evaluations of our work—for external results are all they can see. The quality of our performance is not directly observable. From such a perspective, however, only the duration, and not the intensity, of effort can be measured. Self-managers focus on their performance, and evaluate their returns according to the effort, and not just the time, that they spend in achieving results. They also figure in *internal* reinforcements as part of the returns, instead of just the external rewards that others provide. As a result, their calculations of ROE often diverge significantly from the less fully informed evaluations that others can provide: a self-manager can see progress and find satisfaction where an observer is still awaiting the final results.

MANAGE EFFORT.
THERE IS ONLY ONE WAY
TO GET FROM OBJECTIVES TO RESULTS—
EFFORT.

Objectives tell us where we are headed; results tell us where we have been. What we actually *do*, however, is make a series of efforts that leads from objectives to results. When we manage exclusively by objectives or by results, we ignore the whole range of controllables that determine our results. When we manage by effort, monitoring our performance from step to step in a *sequence* of interim results, we constantly relate an antici-pated end result to our stated preliminary objectives. When we succeed *and* when we fail, we know *why*—and that knowledge can be made the foundation of subsequent success.

MANAGE SELF-CONFIDENCE.
EXPECTATIONS DETERMINE PERFORMANCE,
AND IT'S SELF-CONFIDENCE
THAT DETERMINES EXPECTATIONS.

Self-managers are self-confident. Partly, this is because they are successful—but at the same time, their successes follow from their self-confidence. One direct way to develop self-man-agement abilities is to boost your self-confidence levels. In doing so, you will be able to take on a host of related assumptions and conditioned responses that tend to dissuade us from self-management: the common confusion of self-confidence and arrogance, the acquired tendency to disparage our achieve-ments, and the damaging effects of disapproval, both internal and external.

COMMIT YOURSELF.
CHANGE "I SHOULD" TO "I WILL," AND SET A TIMETABLE.

Commitments to others are often admirable, but they are healthiest and most productive when they proceed from self-commitment, rather than from a passive acceptance of other people's claims and directives. Conditioning makes it easy to replace our deep responsibility to ourselves and our own interests with an endless series of obligations to others. However, genuine self-commitment is not narcissistic or egotistical self-absorption. Making commitments to ourselves, and *keeping them*, is the driving principle of internal reinforcement. It is self-commitment, then, which makes it possible for us to persist against external obstacles, and to attain the goals that we and others value.

DECIDE ONCE: PSYCHOLOGICAL TIME MANAGEMENT.

PUT YOUR ENERGY INTO DOING IT,

NOT

INTO THINKING YOU *SHOULD* DO IT.

Conventional time management, with its schedules and allocations of "clock" time for various activities, is a form of managing by objectives. It sets all kinds of goals, but it has little motivational force, and that little is often of the "push" variety. Time management is usually an attempt to *compensate* for a perceived problem. But "working long" is not the same as working hard. Managing by energy requires a different approach. *Psychological* time—a more precise index of actual energy—is allocated to efforts that proceed from an "I will" rather than an "I should." A personal *decision* carries us into action and towards a goal; we are no longer trying to get away from a previous result.

You Can Choose

The principles of self-management that we have discussed are the key to personal power and productivity. When you apply these principles, you take control of your life, and you take responsibility for your actions. That gives you a sense of power, and it gives you *power* itself—the power to choose, to direct, and to perform your activities. Other people will see that power wherever you exert it: in your job, in your relationships, and in your self-development. And other people will be attracted by that power. Self-managers attract one another, and they also attract those who want to have the same sort of conspicuous satisfaction and success.

When you choose to become a self-manager, you are choosing to be the best that you can be, consistently and reliably. Examine your life: when are you at your best? No doubt, when you are setting your own goals, reaching them, and enjoying your own self-approval and the approval of others. You don't have to *wait* for these moments to happen. You can *create* them, day after day. After reading this book and making a commitment to the principles, you can create an ongoing process of self-management:

- determine your own goals, objectives, and expectations
- figure out what you need to do—the behavior or activity, the strategy or game plan
- make a commitment to the behavior or activity
- *keep* the commitment
- give yourself credit for keeping the commitment

- evaluate your performance of the activity
- evaluate the results
- seek resources for self-improvement and development
- evaluate the overall process, over a period of time, to decide whether to continue it, adjust it, or discontinue it

You can follow this process in every area of activity and ambition, and every day, you can improve your performance, make more of your potential, and get more of the results you want. And when you become a stronger, more effective self-manager, you will become a better leader, a better manager, a better teacher, and a better partner. The choice is yours—and so is the responsibility.

WINNERS ACT ON THEIR OWN AUTHORITY.

TO LEARN MORE ABOUT SELF MANAGEMENT GROUP,

ITS WIDE RANGE OF INDIVIDUAL AND CORPORATE

TRAINING PRODUCTS, AND SELF-MANAGEMENT

WORKSHOPS AND SEMINARS IN YOUR AREA

CALL
416-746-0444

FAX
416-746-6484

E-MAIL
service@selfmgmt.com

WWW
www.selfmgmt.com

SELF MANAGEMENT GROUP
3300 BLOOR STREET WEST, SUITE 650
TORONTO, ONTARIO, M8X 2X2